D1646043

A Guide to the
Adult Support and Protection (Scotland) Act 2007

For

Miss Mary Binnie Speirs (1909–90)
– my primary school teacher,
Larbert Village School

"So much effect, and yet so much a cause –
Where things crowd close she is a space to be in:
She makes a marvel where a nowhere was."

Truth for Comfort (Norman MacCaig)

A Guide to the
Adult Support and Protection
(Scotland) Act 2007

BERT CALDER

DUNDEE UNIVERSITY PRESS
2010

First published in Great Britain in 2010 by
Dundee University Press
University of Dundee
Dundee DD1 4HN

www.dup.dundee.ac.uk

ISBN 978 1 84586 082 0

No natural forests were destroyed to make this product;
only farmed timber was used and replanted.

British Library Cataloguing-in-Publication Data
A catalogue record for this book is available on request from the British Library

Typeset by Waverley Typesetters, Warham, Norfolk
Printed and bound by Bell & Bain Ltd, Glasgow

CONTENTS

FOREWORD

Bert Calder and I were both Mental Health Officers with Central Regional Council in the late 1980s and early 1990s. At that time, we were aware of how inadequate the law was for adults in need of support and the Scots Law Commission highlighted both this and the issue of protection.[1] The Scottish Parliament has now addressed these inadequacies, along with the modernisation of mental health law, since its inception in 1999.

Bert is particularly well qualified to write about the Adult Support and Protection (Scotland) Act 2007. He remains in practice and so every day faces the dilemmas of working with adults at risk of harm. He also has a keen interest in the legal framework for practice and this led him to write a book on the Mental Health (Care and Treatment) (Scotland) Act 2003.

In 2008 Bert was seconded to Adult Care and Support – Change Team in the Scottish Government as a lead professional, which included his involvement in the development of the Code of Practice.

The Adults with Incapacity (Scotland) Act 2000 and the Mental Health (Care and Treatment) (Scotland) Act 2003 which, together with the 2007 Act, make up Scotland's legal framework for adults at risk of harm, have already been amended in response to case law, research and professional opinion. This is because law making is about aspiration and intent: it cannot perceive in advance what the difficulties with it in practice will be. The same is likely to happen with this third statute.

In the meantime, practitioners employed by local authority social work services have to consider its powers and duties. Also, other agencies such as the police and NHS health care trusts have to be knowledgeable about when the Act might apply and when they should make referrals.

This practitioners' guide is therefore timely and its strengths lie in explaining and applying the law to case studies.

A key challenge of this Act is that it focuses on the tricky ethical border between private lives and public concern. Case law

---

[1] Scottish Law Commission Report on *Incapable Adults* (SLC No 151, 1995); Report on *Vulnerable Adults* (SLC No 158, 1997).

and evaluation of practice will eventually clarify when and how local authorities can and should intervene in the private lives of its citizens.

Bert offers a valuable resource for those practitioners who have to work with the Act now.

KATHRYN MACKAY
University of Stirling

PREFACE

I have been a social worker in Falkirk since 1978 – initially with Central Regional Council and then with Falkirk Council. I worked in a generic team for 8 years before becoming a specialist social worker for older people for 4 years and then in a community care team until 2005 when I became a full-time Mental Health Officer. In 2008 my work on the MHO role in the 2003 Act was published.

In 2008 I was seconded to the Adult Care and Support – Change Team in the Scottish Government as a lead professional. My main focus was on identifying gaps in current adult protection research, developing training resources and undertaking a comparison of the 2007 Act, the Adults with Incapacity (Scotland) Act 2000 and the Mental Health (Care and Treatment) (Scotland) Act 2003. I had worked on the Code of Practice Working Group from 2007. This also continued into my secondment. This book follows from my experience with this secondment.

Chapter 1 is a summary of the main concepts in the 2007 Act – the principles; adults at risk; consent and capacity; council officers; and Adult Protection Committees.

Chapters 2–6 discuss the investigations and protection order powers. They are comprehensive and can be read separately, according to need. Chapter 7 deals with court applications for the three protection orders and discusses the kinds of information that may be useful as evidence. This includes general information for the three protection orders followed by specific details applicable to each order. Chapter 8 contains reference information on the amendments to financial powers in the 2000 Act. These amendments are in Pt 2 of the Act. They give councils new powers to take control of an adult with incapacity's finances where harm is an issue. Finally, Chapter 9 attempts to compare and contrast the links and differences among the three main Scottish statutes: incapacity, mental health and adult protection.

At the end of some chapters are questions posed by professionals training in the application of the 2007 Act. The responses are from the author. Also included are some comments from service users and carers who attended a consultation conference entitled "What It Means to Me", organised by the Scottish Government in August 2008.

Appendix 1 contains a glossary. This is a detailed guide to the key terms and phrases in the 2007 Act. It may be useful, therefore, to consult this while reading the main text, in order to refresh knowledge. Appendix 2 lists and discusses the statutory forms of letter pertaining to each power, including court procedures. There is also an information sheet for adults at risk, explaining the details of Pt 1 of the Act. Appendix 3 gives an outline of the Vulnerable Witnesses (Scotland) Act 2004 which may be useful for protection orders where, for example, an adult who is being harmed may have to give evidence.

Given the unique practice-based purpose of this book, I have avoided detailed discussion on the overall development of the 2007 Act. This is a task for the keen-minded researchers in this field.

ACKNOWLEDGEMENTS

I would like to thank the staff of the Adult Care and Support – Change Team, Scottish Government, for their advice and support while researching this book. My thanks also extend to Marion Reddie, Head of Service – Community Care, Falkirk Council; and to the Falkirk Council Community Care Team members in Camelon for reminding me who this book is really for – the services users in our society who have no voice.

I would like to record my personal thanks to the following two professionals for their advice: Lynn Anderson and Douglas Watson.

Among the friends of "worth and choice", I single out Gleb Vulf, who motivated me into writing this book. I also remember, with heart, the encouragement of Anna Ewing, my aunt.

Finally, my thanks go to Kathryn Mackay, Lecturer in Social Work, University of Stirling, for her Foreword; and to Mary Notman, Trainer (Adult Protection), Perth & Kinross Council, for her review of the text.

I acknowledge the permission of the Scottish Government and the Mental Welfare Commission to reproduce legislation and guidance information included in the book.

I would also like to express my general gratitude to other contributors in this field who have been quoted in the book.

The law is stated as at March 2009. Any errors remaining or opinions expressed are my own.

ABBREVIATIONS

Act	Adult Support and Protection (Scotland) Act 2007
adult	an "adult at risk", as defined in s 3 of the Act
APC	Adult Protection Committee
AWI Act	Adults with Incapacity (Scotland) Act 2000
CO	Council Officer, as defined in s 53(1) of the Act
Code of Practice	for local authorities and practitioners exercising functions under Pt 1 of the 2007 Act, amended 15 January 2009[1]
CPN	Community Psychiatric Nurse
GP	general practitioner
JP	justice of the peace
MH Act	Matrimonial Homes (Family Protection) (Scotland) Act 1981
MHO	Mental Health Officer
MWC	Mental Welfare Commission
OPG	Office of the Public Guardian
s	section (referring to a section of the Act or other legislation)
SSI	Scottish Statutory Instrument
subs	subsection (referring to a subsection of the Act or other legislation)
2003 Act	Mental Health (Care and Treatment) (Scotland) Act 2003

---

[1] To be found online at: http://www.scotland.gov.uk/Publications/2009/01/30112831/18

TABLE OF STATUTES

TABLE OF STATUTORY INSTRUMENTS

INTRODUCTION

Adult protection issues are constantly referred to local authority social work services across Scotland where risk assessments are made on a daily basis. This book discusses how to seek solutions in the duties and powers offered to councils by this Act.

The book is intended mainly for those professionals in Scottish councils with a lead role in making the Adult Support and Protection (Scotland) Act 2007 ("the Act") work. More specifically, these responsibilities are invested in what the Act calls a "council officer" ("CO") employed within a local authority social services department. COs come from different professional backgrounds including occupational therapy, nursing and social work. This designation differs from the generic title of "council officer" that is often applied to any local authority employee. The abbreviation "CO" will therefore be used to make this distinction.

The Act gives a CO authority to carry out statutory duties and, where appropriate, to make use of the powers available in Pt 1. The purpose of the CO role is first to investigate circumstances where people, lay and/or professional, believe that an adult in Scotland is at risk of harm; and, second, to provide some means of support and protection for such adults. The legal and practical details required from a CO are explained in each chapter. The term "harm" is interpreted broadly, to include physical, psychological, financial or property harm towards the adult by other people in society. The Act also recognises an adult's self-harm because of the actions of others.

Where there is a need for a protection order, the Act requires the CO to take his assessment of harm to court, using council solicitors to argue a case for different powers. In court, his evidence may be subject to challenge by various parties linked to the harm. The council witness must therefore be confident of his assessments gathered from earlier inquiries and investigations. For some field practitioners this may be daunting and stressful. The presentation of a balanced judgement using the general and guiding principles in the Act will also be scrutinised at court level. This book gives detailed commentary on the legal information required to help such employees and other professionals to meet these challenges. Case studies are used as examples of live evidence.

The wider purpose of this book is to set the Act in the context of other legislation created by the new Scottish Parliament. These are the Adults with Incapacity (Scotland) Act 2000 ("AWI Act") and the Mental Health (Care and Treatment) (Scotland) Act 2003 ("2003 Act"). Each statute shares a number of principles, such as taking into account an adult's past and present wishes and feelings; applying the least restrictive measures; and using the powers to give maximum benefit to an adult subject to the Act. The links with and differences from the two earlier statutes are discussed in Chapter 9. The Act was implemented in 2008. How it is used and its interaction with other statutes will become clearer as practice and case law develops.

The Act is in five parts:

- Part 1 is called "Protection of Adults at Risk of Harm" and outlines the powers and duties available to Scottish councils to implement the Act. These powers are in three sequences: (1) inquiry; (2) investigations; and (3) protection. The first two define which adults in Scotland are "adults at risk" ("adults") and also subject to harm. The third is a legal means to protect such adults by using any of three court protection orders. The responsibility for implementing any of these powers lies largely with the Scottish councils, with the exception of the third protection order (banning order) where they have only a default duty towards the public.

  An inquiry is usually triggered by information given to a Scottish council that an adult is being harmed. The source can be lay individuals or a public body such as the police or a health or social work authority.[1] The council can then progress the results of this inquiry using its investigation powers which include four elements as follows: (1) to visit the adult thought to be harmed; (2) to interview this adult or anyone found with the adult; (3) to have the adult medically examined; (4) to examine any of the adult's records linked to the harm, such as health, finance or social work.

  The use of protection orders involves the Scottish sheriff court system that can grant orders to protect an adult from further serious harm. They are called assessment, removal and banning orders. The definitions of "adult at risk" and "harm" in the Act are used in evidence to grant

---

[1] This may also include referrals from overseas, for example a worried relative.

these orders. These and other key concepts are discussed in Chapter 1.

An assessment order allows a CO to move an adult to a specified place for a private interview within a period of 7 days. A removal order takes the adult from his place of harm to a specified place for up to 7 days in order to prevent further harm. A banning order protects the adult for a period of up to 6 months from any person who has seriously harmed that adult. The Act provides a selection of legal options for banning such a person, including a ban with conditions of no access or of supervised access to the adult. The police have separate powers of arrest attached to a banning order if the person subject to the order breaches these options.

Court warrants are attached to both an investigation visit to the adult and also to the assessment order and the removal order. This allows the police to assist a CO in carrying out his powers.

Finally, the Act requires each council to set up independent Adult Protection Committees to oversee and guide its council and other public bodies in implementing the Act. These committees have a statutory duty to report to the Scottish Government on their activities.

A discussion of Pt 1 will form the main chapters in this book.

- Part 2 amends different parts of the AWI Act in relation to the finance of an adult with incapacity. This is detailed in Chapter 8.

- Part 3 amends and repeals the Social Work (Scotland) Act 1968 in terms of accommodation charges, direct payments, helping adults with incapacity to benefit from social services; and applying social work legislation within the UK.

- Part 4 amends and repeals the 2003 Act.

- Part 5 contains final provisions including ministerial orders and commencement of the Act.[2]

---

[2] See the Explanatory Notes on the Act and also the Scottish Government website on adult support and protection for further discussion on Pts 3–5.

1 KEY CONCEPTS AND FUNCTIONS IN THE ACT

This chapter discusses five main concepts and functions in the Act. Their features will be detailed and, where relevant, followed by commentary on how to use them. The discussion will show how interlinked these concepts are. They are:

- The principles
- Adults at risk
- Consent, capacity and undue pressure
- Council officer
- Adult Protection Committees.

A case study will be used for illustration.

THE PRINCIPLES

The Act begins with two sets of principles – general and guiding principles – which set professional standards for those working with the Act. These include Scottish public bodies and office-holders such as NHS Trusts, local government councils and the police. The principles in this Act also overlap with those of the AWI Act and the 2003 Act, thereby strengthening their importance.

The Code of Practice under Pt 1 of the Act gives the main examples of persons who are *not* bound by the principles. They include the adult who is subject to the Act; the adult's nearest relative; the adult's primary carer (non-paid) or independent advocate; the adult's legal representative; and any guardian or attorney of the adult.[1]

1 General principle on intervention in an adult's affairs

The general principle on intervention in an adult's affairs is that a person may intervene, or authorise an intervention, only if satisfied that the intervention—

(a) will provide benefit to the adult which could not reasonably be provided without intervening in the adult's affairs, and

---

[1] Code of Practice, Chapter 1, para 3.

> *(b) is, of the range of options likely to fulfil the object of the intervention, the least restrictive to the adult's freedom.*

The purpose of the general principle is for any intervention in the Act to adapt to the adult's individual choices and lifestyle, where "benefit" is benefit to the adult and not for other people. An intervention must be used only to improve or stop deterioration in a harming situation. This would be particularly relevant if a removal order were to be used in a situation where the source of harm was not clear, for example in evidence of mutual harm between the adult and another person.[2]

In applying the least restrictive measure, the implication is that any intervention may itself be restrictive for the adult. The professional obligation therefore is to minimise this restriction to a specific issue of harm for the adult. This requires planning an intervention that stops or reduces harm in the adult's life in the least intrusive way possible. The effect of these actions should therefore vary for each individual. The inquiry, investigation and use of protection order stages required by the Act lend themselves to that form of planning, from the least restrictive option of an inquiry to the more restrictive use of protection orders.

The principle of considering the adult's wishes and feelings stems from an adult's right to liberty as described in human rights legislation. This is a fundamental prerequisite of Scots law.[3] At the investigation level, for example, a council officer (CO) must inform the adult of his right to refuse to engage with an interview or with a medical examination. This right also extends to the court in a protection order application where the adult's consent is needed before such an order can be granted. The exceptions to this right are discussed under the heading "Consent, capacity and undue pressure" below, and also in later chapters. The balance between benefit and restriction is therefore threaded throughout discussion of each power in the Act.

The second set of principles, discussed in s 2 below, invites this person-centred approach.

2 Principles for performing Part 1 functions

A public body or office-holder performing a function under this Part in relation to an adult must, if relevant, have regard to—

> *(a) the general principle on intervention in an adult's affairs,*

---

[2] See Chapter 4, where this conflict in benefit is discussed using the case study on Jimmy and Sarah.
[3] See Scottish Human Rights Commission website for further information: http://scottishhumanrights.com/.

(b) the adult's ascertainable wishes and feelings *(past and present)*,

(c) any views of—

    (i) the adult's nearest relative,

    (ii) any primary carer, guardian or attorney of the adult, and

    (iii) any other person who has an interest in the adult's well-being or property,

  which are known to the public body or office-holder,

(d) the importance of—

    (i) the adult participating as fully as possible in the performance of the function, and

    (ii) providing the adult with such information and support as is necessary to enable the adult to so participate,

(e) the importance of ensuring that the adult is not, without justification, treated *less favourably* than the way in which any other adult *(not being an adult at risk)* might be treated in a comparable situation, and

(f) the adult's abilities, background and characteristics *(including the adult's age, sex, sexual orientation, religious persuasion, racial origin, ethnic group and cultural and linguistic heritage)*.

A general starting point could be to give the adult information about the proposed function in the Act, followed by a clear message of participation. The adult should not feel that anything is being imposed without a proper understanding of what the Act is about.[4] This allows the adult to exercise autonomy by discussing his wishes and feelings about benefit and restriction. In short, if the conversation becomes one-sided from any professional towards the adult, the application of the principles has failed.

As an aid to obtaining as much information as possible before using the Act, s 6 states that the council should consider using "appropriate services" to bring about a clearer understanding of the adult's wishes and feelings. The Act singles out independent advocacy services as an example but a known professional or a lay person such as relative or friend could be equally appropriate. The council could utilise the skills of a different professional where the adult has special needs, for example dementia, sensory impairment or communication problems caused by a physical illness or cultural differences. This could include translators for languages other than English.

---

[4] See Appendix 2 for summary information on the Act, to give to adults.

The principle of consulting the views of other people linked to the adult, such as a relative or a friend, or legally if the adult has a welfare guardian through the AWI Act, are standard means of using the Act to investigate and possibly prevent further harm. Their views may also be useful at a later stage as court evidence in applying for a protection order. Some of these parties have legal rights in court, for example to appeal court applications for a banning order (s 51(2)).

The fourth guiding principle, in s 2(e), takes a wider perspective and places the adult within the general Scottish population to include ethnic cultures and sub-cultures. That is why the term "comparable" is used in this section.

Finally, the professional must respect who the adult is by considering their abilities, background and the eight characteristics listed in s 2(d)–(f) above. In short, the support and protection powers in the Act are used to improve how an adult already lives.

CASE STUDY: INA

Ina, aged 60, is single and lives alone in an owner-occupied house. She previously lived with her aunt who is now deceased. Ina has long-standing council tax arrears and has ignored letters and warnings from council staff for over 2 years. The result is a possible eviction notice and reclaiming of the debt. A recent police report to the council also indicates that Ina is being verbally harassed by youths in the area where she shops. This was because of her odd appearance – she wears layers of clothes and looks generally unkempt. However, Ina was unwilling to allow police into her home to discuss this matter.

The finance sections of the council have made a referral to the local authority social services department for a needs assessment before formally evicting Ina. They have requested this assessment to clarify whether Ina has any problems that prevent her from paying the arrears, for example mental health issues. Ina has been allocated a female social worker from the community care team, who knew Ina's aunt. However, Ina keeps the social worker at the door several times in spite of written notice to visit. The medical records show that a GP visited Ina many years ago and assessed her as living in an eccentric way. A male GP tried to visit recently but was refused access.

A case conference was convened, involving the council's housing and legal services departments, to use the Act to try to prevent Ina from becoming homeless. A summary of the powers in the Act was made available so as to focus the discussion. The decision made was to adopt the least restrictive option of a joint visit under s 7 of the Act between the allocated social worker, in her role as a CO, and a consultant in old age psychiatry.

Application of principles to case study

The purpose of the visit was to try to gain access and engage Ina in order to assess her situation and, more importantly, her openness to assistance. In doing this, the CO has to take Ina's current wishes into account. The inquiry information suggests that Ina is isolated and prefers her privacy. To this end, Ina was sent notice of the joint visit. She therefore knew that a doctor would also be present. Initially, Ina kept them both at the door, saying she had been told never to let strangers in. Ina did mention that she had been unwell. The psychiatrist used this comment to offer to look at her medication. Ina then let them in. Ina interpreted this offer as sufficiently beneficial to allow them entry.

Once entry was made, the psychiatrist explained her role and asked questions about Ina's health. The CO recalled visiting Ina's aunt which further helped to gain her confidence. The starting point, however, was Ina's health which in turn later led to a discussion about the Act and the possibility of eviction should Ina not start paying her council tax arrears.

Ina was able to describe her life and financial decisions in a pragmatic way. She did not realise that she owned the house. She thought the house belonged to her late aunt's daughter and this was the reason she had ignored the eviction letters. Ina had her own routines of domestic chores and shopping which had not varied since her aunt's death. She remembered the letters and visits from the social worker and the housing department about the tax arrears. She did not let them in for fear of being evicted.

In the course of the interview, Ina talked about symptoms suggesting mental illness – auditory hallucinations of a threatening nature that disturbed her sleep. These symptoms had been going on for several years. The psychiatrist assessed Ina as possibly having a chronic untreated mental illness. The preliminary diagnosis of a mental disorder was sufficient information in this investigation visit to prevent

Ina's home from being sold. in that the information helped to allow the council to waive Ina's council tax debt and to apply for council tax benefit on her behalf.

Ina wanted to live at home and be treated for her illness. The eviction letters and visits from the council were a source of fear. The CO assured Ina that steps could now be taken to avoid an eviction. This visit alone therefore allayed Ina's fears. There were no significant people in Ina's life for consultation.

The penultimate guiding principle in the Act is to ensure that any action using the legislation does not set the adult apart from others in the population who do not need care and support. In Ina's case the inquiry from the joint visit would probably prevent her threatened eviction. The final guiding principle is linked to the one before in that Ina should not be discriminated against as a result of her age, racial origin, ethnic group and cultural and linguistic heritage. In other words, the fact that Ina was an older person should not discriminate her from other adults in Scotland. Ina's financial and health issues were suitably addressed after this visit by agreeing to separate follow-up appointments by the psychiatrist and also the social worker.

ADULTS AT RISK

3 Adults at risk

(1) "Adults at risk" are adults who—
  (a) are unable to safeguard their own well-being, property, rights or other interests,
  (b) are at risk of harm, and
  (c) because they are affected by disability, mental disorder, illness or physical or mental infirmity, are more vulner-able to being harmed than adults who are not so affected.

(2) An adult is at risk of harm for the purposes of subsection (1) if—
  (a) another person's conduct is causing (or is likely to cause) the adult to be harmed, or
  (b) the adult is engaging (or is likely to engage) in conduct which causes (or is likely to cause) self-harm.

This is the key qualification any adult, such as Ina, must have before the Act can be used for support and protection. The criteria are in a three-pronged test outlined in s 3, where all three conditions must be fulfilled for an adult to be described as an "adult at risk".

The term "harm" is defined in s 53(1) to include all harmful conduct and the following specific categories are listed as a guide: physical, psychological, property, rights or interests and, finally, self-harm precipitated by the conduct of another person. Examples of harm are given in s 53.

The information from the inquiry about Ina only suggested that she might be an "adult at risk" using the s 3(1)(a)–(c) definition:

(a) *Unable to safeguard her property*: Ina not paying her council tax as she was unaware that the house belonged to her and had therefore ignored eviction warnings.

(b) *At risk of harm*: the issue of possible harm had been independently verified by the police using their CCTV system.

(c) *Medical diagnosis*: mental illness of chronic psychosis.

The Act allows for a broad range of evidence to apply the investigation powers. The decision to act on the referral at the inquiry stage is based on the legal test that the council "knows or believes" that an adult may be an "adult at risk" (s 4). In Ina's case, the objective evidence for harm was recorded on the town's CCTV system. This in itself does not prove subjective harm to Ina so the council can only interpret it as a belief.

The other source of evidence was the council's finance department, in terms of Ina's substantial council tax arrears that threatened her eviction, as Ina did not show any effort to prevent her property from being sold to pay off her arrears. The s 7 visit itself, with the CO and the medical practitioner, established that Ina had a mental illness suggesting that she was incapable of responding to these eviction notices.

This is a not uncommon example where information from referrals to a social services department can be patchy. The three-pronged test for an "adult at risk" in s 3, however, can help to justify intervention. In Ina's case the council's duties in the s 4 inquiry led to using the investigation powers in a s 7 visit which then led to a positive outcome in that Ina's council tax arrears and mental illness were addressed with her consent.

The term "conduct" is defined separately in s 53 to include "neglect and other failures to act". This also includes actions that are not planned or deliberate but that have harmful consequences. This may occur, for example, where there is financial dependence on the person caring for the adult or where stress has resulted, for example house sharing and/or external issues such as balancing work and home.

Common risk factors in people who are harmed may include social isolation, communication difficulties, a history of poor relationships and impaired capacity (eg dementia). However, the Act allows a council to interpret "harm" in its broadest sense in order to offer support and protection to a range of adults who can be defined as "adults at risk".[5]

These broad definitions therefore allow the council to consider referrals and apply to them the three-pronged test in s 3. As discussed above, the legal test in s 4 is "knows or believes", which allows the council to consider a wider range of suspected harm. A thorough application of the five guiding principles above should be the context in which a council investigates, beginning with how the adult actually experiences harm[6] (s 4).

The source of harm to an adult may be any individual in the population or the adult themselves, as a consequence of another person's neglect of the adult. Other causes of harm could be professionals employed by public bodies (such as health, social work or independent care agencies). The fact that conduct includes "neglect and a failure to act" implies that any public bodies should have rigorous risk assessments and care plans in place to avoid harm to an "adult at risk".

Adults in formal care settings such as care homes, hospitals or supported accommodation may fulfil only the first and third criteria of s 3. It might be more difficult for a council to apply this Act to such adults even though harm may still be an issue. Examples of harm could be not providing sufficient safeguards to protect an adult with dementia from leaving their home at night; or proper staffing levels in a hospital or in a care home. Institutional harm could also be caused by care provider staff's lack of awareness of what constitutes harm.[7]

The concepts of harm to an adult's property and rights are more straightforward to define, as they relate to objective facts. The other two concepts in s 1(a), of "well-being and other interests", are more subjective and require personal knowledge of the adult and of their circumstances. The guiding principles in s 2 should highlight what those terms mean for the adult personally. In the

---

[5] See the Scottish Government website on training material for adult protection: http://www.scotland.gov.uk/Topics/Health/care/adult-care-and-support/legislation/ASPtraining.

[6] Each council will have procedures in assessing harm. Other readers may wish to look at the paper "Working Together to Improve Adult Protection" by the Joint Improvement Team. This was commissioned by the Scottish Government and published in August 2007.

[7] An example known to the author was of two care assistants tending to an adult with dementia and later playing with the adult's favourite doll by tossing it to each other over her bed.

case study, for example, Ina's well-being and interests involved continuing with her routine at home.

The adult and/or significant others, including professional people, may be able to give specific details on what factors led to harm for the adult (s 2(c)).

The Act lists five separate health-related diagnoses that qualify for inclusion in the last of the three parts of the definition of "adult at risk". The diagnoses include disabilities (undefined); mental disorder; an illness in itself; physical or mental infirmity. The qualification is that these medical diagnoses cause the adult to be more vulnerable to harm than those who do not have such a diagnosis.

The term "mental disorder" is defined in s 328 of the 2003 Act as "mental illness, personality disorder, and learning disability, however caused or manifested". This includes inherited mental illness. The term "disability" has a broader definition that could include physical or psychological trauma. The list of medical conditions becomes even more diffuse by using the old-fashioned term "infirmity", with a dictionary meaning of "physical weakness or debility, frailty".[8] The Act applies the term "infirmity" to physical and mental forms.

The broad scope of these categories of harm, however defined, allows a council to use the Act to support and protect a much larger population compared with the more specific definitions in the AWI Act and the 2003 Act. The court would therefore expect a medical practitioner to assist in giving evidence to substantiate this part of the definition.

The concepts of "vulnerability" and consent to any intervention therefore become more crucial in order to avoid discrimination (s 3(1)(c) and s 35). The Act rightly leaves this ultimately for the court to decide. It follows, then, that caution by council solicitors taking instructions from social work staff should not put a stop to potential court applications.

CONSENT, CAPACITY AND UNDUE PRESSURE

Obtaining consent

Consent is required from any adult subject to an investigation by the CO in either an interview or a medical examination. The adult must also give consent in both a court application and the ongoing implementation of the three protection orders (s 35(1) and (2)).

---

[8] *Collins English Dictionary* (2000, reprinted 2007).

The consent must be informed by knowledge of the Act and the ways in which it will benefit and be least restrictive to the adult. In other words, the CO has to gauge whether the adult is giving informed consent. The Act also allows applications for a banning order from the adult and any person entitled to occupy the same place as the adult. These applicants have to apply the same consent issues as for the council.

The Act lists four conditions for the CO to carry out a visit under s 7. They are:

(i)   to visit at reasonable times;
(ii) to state the purpose of the visit and to produce authorisation;
(iii) to examine any place, take any other person and any equipment to fulfil the purpose of the visit;[9] and
(iv) not to use force except without a warrant (s 36).

The second and third provisions allow the CO to make a judgement on the adult's ability to consent. If this is in doubt, then the third provision allows another person (such as a health professional) to assist with the visit. This is different from a medical examination under s 9, the purpose of which is to establish the presence of harm.

In the case study on Ina above, the visit was an investigation using a CO's visiting powers under s 7. The purpose was to establish whether Ina was an "adult at risk" and what could be done to protect her from harm. Ina was aware of the eviction threat through letters and attempted visits from the housing department. The psychiatrist told Ina that she would visit her alone later, to give her a check-up in privacy. The CO too could visit Ina, this time in her role as a social worker, to assist her in completing a council tax form. Arguably, the harm element for Ina was being harassed by youths in the town but the application of the Act triggered off other forms of care and support.

The adult should have sight of the terms in each intervention before consenting orally and, where appropriate, in writing. The need for written consent may vary according to the type of action being pursued under the Act. For example, if an advocacy worker or trusted friend is present then oral consent may be more appropriate, in contrast to written consent for the more formal court applications. Where consent is in writing, the CO could consider having the adult's consent witnessed by the same

---

[9] Examples of equipment might be to assist communication where the adult had a sensory impairment. In other cases, a translator or a specialist in communication for, say, an adult with special needs may be appropriate.

advocacy worker or a trusted friend in order to strengthen the application.[10]

Consent is withheld

If an adult's informed consent is not given for an interview, for a medical examination or for a court application for any of the protection orders, the CO cannot proceed. The adult can, however, consent to parts of both the interview and the medical examination (s 8(2); s 9(2)). Reasons for an adult not giving informed consent could be a sense of loyalty, where family are involved; the adult may come from a cultural background which does not complain; fear that complaining will make things worse; and the fear that he may have to go into care.

In terms of a protection order application, the sheriff has to be satisfied that the adult consents to the application. If the adult does not consent, the sheriff has to assess whether there is sufficient evidence to fulfil the legal test of "undue pressure" using s 35(3) (see the heading "Undue pressure" below). The sheriff is therefore not assessing the adult's capacity but instead whether or not his informed consent can be disregarded.

Consent and incapacity

A CO should explore the issue of capacity to give consent at the investigation visit (s 7). For interviews, the Code of Practice provides a helpful list of questions to use in assessing the adult's capacity.[11] Where there is doubt about capacity, however, the provisions in s 36(3)(b)(i) allow for another professional to visit and in this circumstance to assess for a lack of capacity to consent to any intervention in the Act.

In any investigation, the CO should presume capacity and then provide proof of incapacity. If a protection order were being sought then the evidence for an adult's incapacity would come from a medical practitioner, much the same as for the "adults with incapacity" legisation.[12] The court then has to decide on the consent issue – whether the adult has sufficient or insufficient capacity to consent to the order being pursued. If there is sufficient capacity, the sheriff has to decide whether that refusal to consent

---

[10] Code of Practice, Chapter 9, para 21 has useful guidance on approaching the consent issue.

[11] *Ibid*, Chapter 6, para 8.

[12] However, it may be more appropriate for a medical practitioner to visit the adult alone rather than more formally with the council officer in a s 7 visit. If there is resistance, a warrant under s 37(1)(a) can then be used to carry out this visit.

is due to "undue pressure" (s 35(3)). If the adult has insufficient capacity to give consent, the Code of Practice clearly states that the sheriff will require this evidence of incapacity.[13]

If the adult does not have capacity to consent, it may be that he has made legal provision for another person to consent on his behalf. This would be done using the range of consent powers available in the AWI Act where the person delegated to use these powers is called a "proxy". These records are stored by the Office of the Public Guardian (OPG), currently based in Falkirk. These powers range from a power of attorney to guardianship orders. The Code of Practice advises that a CO should make standard inquiries to the OPG if such powers exist.[14]

If the adult has incapacity, the intervention will vary according to the kind of harm being committed. For example, for financial harm, Pt 2 of the Act now gives the council more powers to intervene. The council could consider a guardianship order using the AWI Act. If the adult is in imminent danger from harm, then a removal order using either this Act or the 2003 Act could be considered.[15]

In sum, no council can walk away from a situation where it "knows or believes" that a person is an adult at risk, with or without capacity as the case may be. The council still has a duty to protect that person's "well-being, property or financial affairs".[16] The adult who lacks capacity to consent must be treated no less favourably than other adults at risk.

Test of capacity

The AWI Act, in s 1(6), lists five criteria the presence of which implies that the adult has incapacity. This could therefore be a useful guide for the CO to use in the first instance at a s 7 visit. As discussed above, the Code of Practice, in Chapter 6, para 8, offers useful guidance on assessing capacity as opposed to incapacity. The Act includes further provisions within a visit that could be used to evidence incapacity, such as the CO taking with him a health professional (s 36(3)(b)(i)).

As a guide, the definition of incapacity in s 1(6) of the AWI Act is where the adult is incapable of any one of the following:

---

[13] Code of Practice, Chapter 11, para 14
[14] This advice is in different chapters of the Code of Practice: Chapter 9, para 11 (assessment orders); Chapter 10, para 15 (removal orders); Chapter 11, para 14 (banning orders).
[15] Section 293 of the 2003 Act applies to adults with a mental disorder. The adult may also require care and treatment using civil compulsory orders.
[16] Section 4 powers apply to any department in the council. The social work department would be the means of co-ordinating inquiries.

(a) acting;
(b) making decisions;
(c) communicating decisions;
(d) understanding decisions; or
(e) retaining the memory of decisions.

The AWI Act Code of Practice makes it clear that the issue of capacity is not a global one.[17] The capacity being assessed would be whether or not the adult understands the purpose of any intervention in terms of the Act.[18] The legal test of incapacity would therefore have to be determined by a sheriff. He may choose to use the AWI Act definition of incapacity in s 1(6) above.[19]

If a proxy has been appointed under the AWI Act and has specific powers then he is allowed to give consent on the adult's behalf. He should be present at the interviews, provided that he is not the suspected source of harm. The council too can seek welfare powers in a guardianship order using the AWI Act.

Undue pressure: s 35

This concept is specifically related to court applications for protection orders. If the applicant proves that another person is prohibiting the adult from consenting to the application, he can use the "undue pressure" test to have that consent ignored by the sheriff (s 35(3)). Proof of undue pressure is not required where an adult lacks capacity to consent. The use of medical evidence to prove incapacity would be a substitute.[20] The Act describes one relationship that can cause undue pressure being from someone in whom the adult has confidence and trust but who nevertheless is harming the adult. If this trust did not exist, the adult would then want to give consent to the protection order (s 35(4)).

In contrast, undue pressure could be from a person who the adult does not trust and who is harming him, for example by using threats. It could also be from a person not suspected of harming the adult, for example someone placing undue pressure on him not to consent in order to cover up for someone else (s 35(5); Code of Practice, Chapter 9, paras 22–24). The Act also allows for

---

[17] AWI Act Code of Practice for local authorities exercising functions under the Act, para 2.28.5, p 27; para 3.20 onwards to para 3.46.

[18] Scottish Government, "Communication and Assessing Capacity – a guide for social work and health care staff" (2008).

[19] This is speculation on the author's part, as there is no specific reference to the term "incapacity" in the Act. The Code of Practice, Chapter 11, para 14 uses the phrase "evidence of lack of capacity".

[20] This is repeated for all protection orders in the Code of Practice. See n 14 above for references.

undue pressure coming from a person who is not harming the adult, such as a neighbour, carer or other person (s 35(5)).[21]

The term has two subjective components, "undue" and "pressure", which will vary for each adult. However, the use of the principles should give a CO more insight into an adult's wishes and how he reacts to information about the proposed intervention. In considering the reasons for the undue pressure, the CO could ask open questions which may elicit responses suggesting negative consequences to the adult himself, such as anticipated threats or intimidations or a fear of being alone and no longer being supported. Other non-verbal clues could be the adult not talking when certain people are present; not being allowed to be alone with the CO; or the adult's body language suggesting inhibition.[22]

The guiding principles require the CO to consider the views of people significant to the adult, such as a close relative or perhaps a trusted professional. The evidence for "undue pressure" can then be confirmed or otherwise from this information. If "undue pressure" is suspected, the CO then has to locate the source or sources of this harm towards the adult.

The test of "undue pressure" must relate to how the adult usually reacts to persuasion from the person allegedly pressuring him. This may involve a separate interview with that person, using the s 8 interview power.[23] Alternative sources of information may, however, be more useful, given any person's right to refuse to answer questions.

COUNCIL OFFICER (CO): s 52(1)

A CO is an employee of the local authority social services department, with specific duties and powers, given in the Act. These powers are prescribed by Scottish Statutory Instruments (SSIs), also termed "orders" in s 78 of the Act. These are secondary pieces of legislation to each Act that give specific details about how it will work. They are named and then referenced by year and number. The CO role is described in the Adult Support and Protection (Scotland) Act 2007 (Restriction on the

---

[21] The Code of Practice, Chapter 9, paras 23 and 24 discusses these types of situations.

[22] Council procedures will have their own checklist of signs of undue pressure. I am grateful for sight of the Perth & Kinross Council draft adult protection procedures, for reference.

[23] The council officer is restricted to interviewing any adult found in a place being visited under s 7. In other words, he cannot pursue an interview beyond the adult's place.

Authorisation of Council Officers) Order 2008 (abbreviated to SSI 2008/306).

The SSI distinguishes between two types of CO who perform separate duties in terms of the Act:

(1) *social service workers* – investigations only (ss 7–10);
(2) *social workers; occupational therapists; nurses* – investigations and protection orders (ss 7–10; 11, 14, 16 and 18).[24]

Both types of CO must be registered with their professional bodies in addition to being council employees and having at least 12 months' post-qualifying experience of identifying, assessing and managing adults at risk. The Regulation of Care (Scotland) Act 2001, under s 77 "Interpretation", distinguishes a social worker from a social services worker. The basic distinction is as follows:

- *social workers*: with an accredited qualification in social work;
- *social services workers*: employed in the provision of (or in managing the provision of) a care service. They are therefore not registered as social workers.

The Act allows the CO to interview an adult jointly with any person accompanying the CO.[25] The Act widens the scope of people who can assist the CO to carry out an interview using s 8. The use of the non-qualifying term "person" could include another council employee or anyone from another profession (s 8(1)). This contrasts with the medical examination power, where the person accompanying the CO is a health professional.[26] Furthermore, this examination of the adult must be in private and, where appropriate, exclude the CO.

With an assessment order, however, the Act allows either the CO or a council nominee to interview the adult in a private place (s 11(1)(a)). The same choice applies for removal orders (s 14(1)(a)). These nominees can be from any profession and would not be subject to the same training requirements as a CO (s 11(1)(a); s 14(1)(a)). This delegation power seems paradoxical, given the key role of the CO in other parts of the Act.

---

[24] Sections 7–10 include visits, interviews, medical examinations and examination of records. Section 11 (assessment orders); s 14 (removal orders); s 16 (right to move adult at risk); and s 18 (protection of moved person's property).

[25] Code of Practice, Chapter 6, para 9.

[26] The term "health professional' is defined in s 52 of the Act as a doctor, nurse, midwife or any other type of individual specified by the Scottish Ministers by statutory instrument.

Good practice would suggest that joint work with a council nominee would be the norm. This is the case for a Mental Health Officer in the 2003 Act when working with police or health professionals.

ADULT PROTECTION COMMITTEES (APCs)[27]

APCs are included in the Act under s 42. Each council must establish them in order to perform four main functions as follows:[28]

(1) review procedures and practice within their council;
(2) give information and advice to any public body on their function of safeguarding adults;
(3) carry out or encourage training for employees from any public body in their function of safeguarding adults;
(4) any other function specified by the Scottish Ministers.

Public bodies and office-holders represent an APC. A convener who is independent from the council chairs each APC (s 43(6)). Each APC can regulate its own procedure but must allow attendance by the Mental Welfare Commission (MWC); the Office of the Public Guardian (OPG); the Care Commission; and any other public body or office-holder specified by the Scottish Government (s 44).

APCs are entitled to request information linked to their functions from any public body or office-holder (s 45). The convener must provide a general report on the exercise of their functions. This is expected on a 2-year cycle (s 46).[29] Public bodies listed in s 42(3) include:

(a) the council;
(b) the Care Commission;
(c) the relevant Health Board;
(d) the chief constable of the police force maintained in the council's area;
(e) any public body or office-holder as the Scottish Minister may by order specify.

---

[27] Scottish Government, "Draft Guidance on Adult Protection Committees" (21 May 2008) (available on its website only).

[28] The Act uses the singular term "council" but, given the varying populations in Scotland, some councils have collaborated to form APCs.

[29] The 2-year cycle officially started when the Act was implemented in full from October 2008 but APCs were not then properly convened across some parts of Scotland.

QUESTIONS FROM PROFESSIONALS[30]

1. There is a legal duty under s 36(1) and (2)(b) for a CO, when visiting, to show authorisation to visit and advise the adult that he does not need to answer questions. If the affected adult lacks capacity to understand this but you believe he may be able to provide information (for example he had a bruise to the face and could be asked "What happened to your face?"), can such a question be properly asked, perhaps with an advocate present?

RESPONSE

The Act suggests in s 6(2) the use of "appropriate services", singling out independent advocacy services as a means to overcome this issue. If the adult lacks capacity then would you expect a straightforward reply? What the Act does is to focus on the concepts of "adults at risk" and "harm". If the initial visit yields the facts that the adult has incapacity and cannot give an account of the source of his harm, for example a bruise, but it is still apparent, then formal protection may be required. The results of a joint CO/health professional visit may then develop from "information" to "evidence" for use in protection orders.

2. Section 5 – the duty to co-operate with a council making inquiries. Does it extend to English/Welsh/Northern Irish councils/police/health? There is no reference to this, so it seems not?

RESPONSE

The legal duty of co-operation with other councils applies only to Scotland. However, if an "adult at risk" were moved to or from another part of the United Kingdom would it not be good practice in any way to adopt current practice and share information? The issue of consent would also be a factor. Perhaps the Adult Protection Committees for each council can offer procedures for information sharing both within and beyond Scotland.

---

[30] This is taken from a selection of questions raised by professionals' training sessions on the Act. They came from Ian Kinsley, Care Training Matters Ltd. The phraseology of the original questions is intact but is followed by current responses from this author.

3. Does inquiring and collating information using ss 5 and 10 about an "adult at risk" extend to an alleged harmer?

RESPONSE

I agree that the issue of access to information of a third party is fraught with difficulty. This is a civil action designed to support and protect an "adult at risk". The focus of the information would be the adult's circumstances. The relevance of the alleged harmer's circumstances would therefore stem from this inquiry. However, the CO can interview the alleged harmer using his powers under s 8(1) but only if the latter is found in the same place as the adult but still subject to refusal rights in s 8(2).

The guidance on court applications in Chapter 7 of this book suggests that the CO lists those unanswered questions for the court. The sheriff then has an option to appoint a safeguarder, using s 41(6), to make further inquiries. The sheriff, using his discretionary powers in s 41(7), can direct the safeguarder to interview the suspected harmer in private. With banning orders, the subject of the order too has a legal right to challenge the application. It is then for the sheriff to decide whether the evidence from any party is admissible.

If this inquiry information suggests that a crime has been committed by the suspected harmer, it would be a starting point for the police to investigate and build evidence for prosecution.

4. The Code of Practice, in Chapter 5 on visits, seems to militate against a visit and/or interview taking place without a CO. If the referral is one of concern in a hospital, the consultant and staff nurse may be seen as the best professionals to interview the adult. Is this interview covered by the Act? It is relevant in so much as there can be many allegations about nursing staff in hospitals – if these were now to be reported to the council (as per s 5(3)), the option of a health-only response would now seem not possible, or at least not possible as a s 4 inquiry.

RESPONSE

If a hospital team come across suspected harm then they would normally use their own procedures to deal with it. The co-operation principle in s 5(3) states that a public body

> *must report the "facts and circumstances of the case" to the council about any measures that need to be taken to protect an "adult at risk" from harm.*
>
> *These public bodies therefore need to know what the powers in the Act are. If action is needed, a CO would then be part of the investigation, using a s 7 visit and possibly too a s 8 interview with the adult. This could also include the alleged harmer, using the same interview powers. If a medical examination has already been done, that would be part of the hospital's duty to co-operate with the council under s 5(1)(f). The council too can use its power in examination of records under s 10, to obtain medical information about the harm.*
>
> *At a policy level, it is for the council's APC to give information or advice, or make proposals, to any public body on the exercise of its functions that relate to harm issues. It may be that APCs decide that all incidents of harm within any public body must be reported and then investigated by the council (s 42(1)(b)).*

VIEWS OF SERVICE USERS AND CARERS[31]

- *The Act in general*: social work services will standardise procedures rather than tailor them to the individual's needs.

- *Disability issues*: s 3(1)(c): definition of "adult at risk" – disabled people could be treated differently from others, particularly those with capacity.

- *Assessment and protection planning*: risk assessment may make professionals more risk averse, resulting in service users leading more limited lives – "overprotective staff and parents". More than one social worker should make an assessment and/or decision.

- *Support services*: s 6(2): domestic violence – there are few, if any, accessible refuges for disabled women. There are none for men. People need options to enable them to make proper choices. If the options are few, then the choices are fewer.

---

[31] This is a selection of concerns expressed in relation to different functions of the Act, expressed at a conference for service users and carers to comment on the Act, held by the Scottish Government on 21 August 2008 and called "What It Means to Me".

- *Co-operation, information sharing and disclosure of records*: s 5.
  - Unclear what voluntary groups' legal duties are if they are publicly funded. Could place too much responsibly on the voluntary sector.
  - The adult may not wish certain information to be shared or even be aware that it is happening.
  - Fear that we are all "heading towards Big Brother".
- *Inquiries and investigations*: ss 4 and 7–10: professionals may jump to conclusions. "Things aren't always what they seem." An inquiry or investigation could cause the situation to deteriorate.

2 COUNCIL DUTIES AND POWERS

This chapter summarises the powers and duties of a council throughout Pt 1 of the Act. This will be followed by a discussion of the inquiries and investigation powers. The case study in Chapter 1 on Ina will be continued, given the overlap in applying the principles to investigations.

COUNCIL DUTIES AND POWERS – SUMMARY

The Act describes specific interventions to allow a council to support and protect an adult from harm. These interventions are of two types: (1) duties, which focus on establishing whether or not an adult is being harmed and deciding what can be done to prevent further harm; and (2) powers, which are used actually to protect the adult from further harm. Council duties are mandatory, whereas the use of powers is an option. The extent to which a council fulfils a duty will depend on professional judgement.[1]

The Act uses the term "protection" in relation to both duties and powers but there is also an implicit duty to support the adult in benefiting from any parts of the Act being used. This includes financial issues in Pt 2. The Act prescribes who can undertake these powers and duties while the Code of Practice provides details as to how any authorised person should act in relation to these. They are listed below, with the relevant legal reference in brackets.

Council duties:

- Respond to inquiries about an adult's well-being, property or financial affairs for an adult who may be at risk of harm (s 4).
- Provide appropriate services to an adult subject to an inquiry, for example independent advocacy services (s 6).
- Other public bodies and office-holders, including councils, have a duty to co-operate with the councils and with each other where harm is believed or known to have taken place (s 5(3)).

---

[1] Section 52; Code of Practice, Chapter 2, paras 3 and 4 discuss these distinctions in more detail.

Council powers:

- Visit any adult at any place to inquire whether it needs to do anything to protect an adult at risk from harm (s 7).
- Interview or arrange a medical examination of an adult suspected of being harmed (ss 8 and 9, respectively).
- Apply for any of the three protection orders known as assessment, removal or banning orders (ss 11, 14 and 19, respectively).
- Use a warrant to enter any place to visit under s 7, or use with either an assessment order or a removal order (s 37).
- Establish Adult Protection Committees alone or with other councils (optional) (s 42).

INQUIRIES AND INVESTIGATIONS

Inquiries

4 Council's duty to make inquiries

A council must make inquiries about a person's well-being, property or financial affairs if it knows or believes—

    (a) that the person is an adult at risk, and

    (b) that it might need to intervene (by performing functions under this Part or otherwise) in order to protect the person's well-being, property or financial affairs.

Any referral about suspected harm should be made to the local authority through its social services department. Referral could be from another public body or an individual. The council, in consultation with other professionals, for example police, health and housing, using its s 5 co-operation duties (see below), then does an initial inquiry. This could be by telephone or more formally in a multi-disciplinary meeting, to gather more information to decide on action using the council powers available in the Act.

The criterion for inquiring rests on the concept "knows or believes" in s 4, giving the council a broad scope for taking action or no action. The knowledge gathered from a referral in itself could have limited value but become stronger if this is developed into possible scenarios of harm. In Ina's case study, for example, the knowledge is of her non-payment of council tax and not responding to letters from housing. Ina also refused access to the social worker, leading the council to "believe" there was some reason other than wilfulness causing her to ignore the warning about losing her house. For other referrals, the need to intervene may be met by parallel legislation where specific health details are already known, for example an adult with a mental impairment resulting in incapacity or a mental disorder. The AWI Act or the 2003 Act should therefore be considered in tandem.

If, after a referral was made, the decision was to take no action, the following checklist list should be considered before closing an inquiry:[2]

(i) adult has been spoken to alone;
(ii) adult's place has been visited;
(iii) relevant professionals' views have been sought;
(iv) adult's welfare is safeguarded by using a risk assessment.

Co-operation from public bodies: s 5

This follows from the council's duty to make inquiries where it may need further information or active co-operation from other professional bodies. Similarly, the public body has to inform the council if it knows or believes that an adult is being harmed and is in need of protection.

The Act describes this process as reporting the "facts and circumstances" of the case to the council (s 5(3)). The list of public bodies includes the Mental Welfare Commission; the Care Commission; the Public Guardian; all councils; chief constables of police forces; the relevant Health Board. They also have to work with each other where appropriate (s 5(1), and (2)(b)).

Voluntary groups and independent care providers are not included in this prescribed list but it is expected that they will agree to local protocols to have a duty to inform their local council of suspected harm. However, the Act allows APCs to co-opt representatives recommended by the Care Commission with "skills and knowledge" relevant to the functions in the Act. This will probably include non-statutory agencies (s 43(3)).

Providing advocacy and other services: s 6

The Act applies the need for an adult to have this service if an inquiry suggests that the adult might require further intervention to protect them from harm. This would initially be the s 7 visit and later the s 8 interview. Although not stated, support from an appropriate service may also be relevant when applying and implementing the protection orders.[3]

---

[2] This list is taken from the Falkirk Council harm procedures which the author helped to compile.

[3] The statutory court procedures for all protection order applications include the adult's right to be accompanied by a friend, a relative or any representative chosen by the adult (s 41(5)).

The Act stresses the importance of considering an independent means of support as a safeguard for an adult and highlights the independent advocacy services in s 6(2). Age Concern promoted this idea of mediation in the run-up to the Act as an example of "appropriate services". The definition of an "appropriate service" will depend on the adult's circumstances. For example, where property or finance is under investigation, this could be a solicitor or, for welfare, the allocation of a care manager employed by the social work department.

In the case study in Chapter 1, Ina's appropriate service could be the independent advocacy service or someone who knows about her financial situation. According to the guiding principle of participation in s 2(d), Ina should be given some choice in the matter.

VISITS

7 *Visits*

> *(1) A council officer may enter any place for the purpose of enabling or assisting a council conducting inquiries under section 4 to decide whether it needs to do anything (by performing functions under this Part or otherwise) in order to protect an adult at risk from harm.*
>
> *(2) A right to enter any place under subsection (1) includes a right to enter any adjacent place for the same purpose.*

A visit is a legal investigation to carry out an assessment in relation to an "adult at risk" of harm. These terms are discussed in Chapter 1. This power allows a CO to enter any place for this purpose. The place visited is not specific to accommodation. The Act interprets "place" to mean "the area where the person is for the time being" (s 53). This means virtually anywhere in Scotland. The scope of this investigation power is therefore substantial.

The Code of Practice lists examples of places such as the homes of relatives, day centres, places of education, residential accommodation, or hospitals or other medical facilities.[4] The Code of Practice suggests that good practice would be advance notification of the visit. The qualification added is "where this would not be prejudicial to the safety or welfare of the adult at risk". Visits should be timed for when the adult or other relevant people can be visited in private. This therefore may mean out-of-hours or weekend arrangements.[5]

---

[4] Code of Practice, Chapter 5, paras 9, 10 and 13.

The safeguards for any person being visited are listed in s 36 as follows:

(1) to visit at reasonable times;
(2) to state the object of the visit and to produce authorisation;
(3) to examine any place and take any other person and any equipment into that place;
(4) to perform any other action in this Act or otherwise which is reasonably required to fulfil the object of the visit.[6]

An example of equipment could be for an adult with special needs. A specialist could be present to ease communication with such an adult, for example a sensory impairment social worker, or a community nurse in learning disability, depending on the nature of the adult's special needs.

Section 7(1) does not state whether another person can accompany the CO. This is only included in s 8(1) for an interview power. It is assumed therefore that an interview would follow. This opens up the Act and the use of other parallel legislation to supplement the purpose of a visit. In Ina's case, a psychiatrist was used to establish mental disorder. The person accompanying the CO may be a co-worker to observe and record the visit or a professional related to the nature of the suspected harm, for example a bank official or health professional. A layperson known to the adult could also be present to assist the CO in assessing the risk of harm to the adult. This is well detailed in the Code of Practice.[7]

If either the adult or another person refuses entry, then a "warrant for entry" can be sought at the local court for where the adult is living or by using a justice of the peace in cases of urgency. Warrant applications are discussed in Chapters 6 and 7.

If protection is needed, the council has to consider what legal options are appropriate to progress with this or with other legislation. The interventions in this Act are interviews, medical examinations, and examination of records. These powers are discussed below. The other main interventions are the three protection orders known as assessment, removal and banning orders. The protection orders are discussed separately in Chapters

---

[5] Code of Practice, Chapter 5, para 15.
[6] This opens up the Act and other parallel legislation to supplement the purpose of a visit. In Ina's case, a psychiatrist was used to establish mental disorder.
[7] Code of Practice, Chapter 5, paras 6, 7 and 8.

3, 4 and 5. These powers can be used in any order, depending on the adult's circumstances.

The CO can advise his council that no action is required or that more than one form of legal action is appropriate. For example, in the case study in Chapter 1, a housing official may have to accompany the CO to explain and help Ina to complete a council tax benefit claim. The CO can fulfil these purposes in any of the following three ways:

(i)   other agencies assist the council with their inquiries;

(ii) the council has to decide whether the adult is an "adult at risk", using the three-pronged test in s 3. This is done by a s 7 visit and subsequent use of ss 8–10;

(iii) establishing what action is needed. This could be protection orders or other legislation.

INTERVIEWS

8 Interviews

(1) *A council officer, and any person accompanying the officer, may interview, in private, any adult found in a place being visited under section 7.*

(2) *An adult interviewed under this section is not required to answer any question (and the adult must be informed of that fact before the interview starts).*

(3) *The power given by subsection (1) applies regardless of whether the sheriff has granted an assessment order authorising the council officer to take the person to another place to allow an interview to be conducted.*

An interview is a legal power by a CO to pursue an investigation of harm towards an adult. Where appropriate, the interview extends to any person found in the same place as the adult. The interview can also take place where an adult has been taken to another place using an assessment order. The precursor for an interview is a visit under s 7 to establish the need for further investigations. If harm is suspected or known to have taken place already, the CO should also plan with the adult what action can be done to prevent further harm. The following is a suggested approach by the council officer:[8]

(i)   establish adult's views as to whether or not they are being harmed and by whom;

---

[8] These guidelines are expanded from the Code of Practice, Chapter 6, para 4.

(ii) discuss, with the adult's consent, what action is appropriate to prevent further harm;

(iii) interview other adults who may know of the harm or be the cause of the harm.

The place of interview can be any place where the adult is being visited and is not confined to a habitual residence.

As discussed in the investigation visit, an appropriate service such as an independent advocacy service should be a consideration in these interviews.

The qualification for an interview is that any other person eligible to be interviewed has to be "found" in the same place as the adult. This can be any person either in the premises or linked to the adult's life, professionally, by family, friendship, or in any other way.

The adult's rights in their interview are to be informed by the CO of their right to refuse to answer all or any of the questions. This legal right persists for the adult when interviewed in a different place using an assessment order (s 8(3)).

The general and guiding principles in ss 1 and 2 should also be observed as standard practice in any interview:

- seeking informed consent from the adult;
- promoting the adult's participation;
- conducting an interview that is least restrictive and beneficial;
- providing information and support to allow full participation.

In terms of privacy, the CO must decide, based on the objectives of the interview, whether or not an adult should be interviewed with another person present. The Act allows the CO this discretion, using the phrase "any person accompanying the officer" (s 8(1)). This should be decided in consultation with the adult. It may be necessary that a series of interviews should be carried out, depending on the kind of information gleaned from the first interview. This would then allow the CO to decide what other professional should accompany them, for example if financial harm is an issue or a threatened assault from another person. A medical practitioner may therefore not be the most appropriate person to be involved in initial interviews.[9]

---

[9] The Adult Protection Committees in each council may decide, for example, on protocols for joint health or police interviews (s 42(1)(a)).

Specialists in trauma, such as a psychologist or a speech and language therapist to assess an adult's communication skills, may be a useful resource for the CO to use in s 8 interviews.

MEDICAL EXAMINATION

9 Medical examinations

(1) Where—
   (a) a council officer finds a person whom the officer knows or believes to be an adult at risk in a place being visited under section 7, and
   (b) the officer, or any person accompanying the officer, is a health professional,

that health professional may conduct a private medical examination of the person.

(2) A person must be informed of the right to refuse to be examined before a medical examination is carried out (whether under this section or in pursuance of an assessment order).

(3) The power given by subsection (1) applies regardless of whether the sheriff has granted an assessment order authorising the council officer to take the person to another place to allow a medical examination to be conducted.

A medical examination allows a health professional to examine a person suspected of being an "adult at risk" of harm. This is done in private where the adult is being visited, or elsewhere using an assessment order. The purpose and reasons for a medical examination is to assist the CO with inquiries about the nature of suspected harm as follows:

   (i) to assess the adult's need for immediate medical treatment;
   (ii) to provide evidence of harm, either for a criminal inquiry or to apply for any protection orders;
   (iii) to assess the adult's physical health needs or mental capacity.

The health professionals legally entitled to examine an adult are a doctor; a nurse; a midwife; or any other type of individual of a class prescribed by the Scottish Ministers (s 52(2)). Examples of circumstances of a medical examination could be physical injury allegedly from another person; disclosure of sexual abuse; adult subject to physical or self-neglect; adult injured with no prior treatment having been sought. Where mental capacity is an issue, a psychiatric assessment may be appropriate.

The adult has a right to refuse any part of the medical examination. Given that the definition of "harm" includes mental disorder, the adult may not have the capacity to consent to a medical examination. If this is the case, the adult still has a right to support and protection using this Act or other legislation. The CO and the health professional should jointly make a risk assessment about the adult's safety. If this in jeopardy then a removal order may be appropriate.

Before taking this decision, the CO should contact the Office of the Public Guardian (OPG) to check whether a proxy has powers under the AWI Act to consent on behalf of the adult. This point is well made in the Act's Code of Practice.[10]

EXAMINATION OF RECORDS: s 10

Examination of records is a legal power that permits a CO to obtain written or e-mailed copies of health, finance or other records relating to an adult known or believed to be at risk of harm. The Act uses the term "other records" to allow the council to extend this power if necessary. In short, access to any source of information to support and protect an adult at risk of harm is also permissible in law regardless of whether there is a formal contract with the council. This could, for example, include voluntary organisations or provider services. Where appropriate, this power also extends beyond care agencies to banks, businesses of any kind and also public bodies.[11]

The purpose of the examination of an adult's records is to allow the CO to decide what, if any, legal measures are necessary to prevent further harm to the adult (s 10(4)).

The Code of Practice suggests that authorisation for such approaches within the council should come from a designated senior officer. They would have liaised with record-holders whose information is more likely to be needed in an investigation, for example health professionals using the Community Health Partnerships within each council area.[12]

This information can be obtained during a visit or at any other time. Section 10(2) affords the CO the option of returning to the adult's place for further information, or to pursue this power by

---

[10] Code of Practice, Chapter 7, para 6. This could be part of the inquiry stage in s 4.

[11] *Ibid*, Chapter 8, paras 9 and 10.

[12] *Ibid*, Chapter 8, para 21.

direct contact with the record-holder. In the latter case, a request can be in writing, by fax or using an e-mail (s 10(6)).

The implication for all record-holders is relevance and accuracy of information about an adult being investigated by a council. These records could be used as evidence in court when applying for a protection order. Any party in the court procedure for protection orders may therefore cite the authors of these records as court witnesses, using their legal rights under s 41(4).

The adult's consent should be sought in most cases by using the adult's signature on standard consent forms. In this way, it may help the record-holder to disclose the information alongside the council's s 10 statutory powers. This consent should be waived only in special circumstances. The Code of Practice is helpful in steering the CO through three consent scenarios where the adult's consent can be waived, as follows:[13]

(1) It is in the public interest to seek disclosure. This is linked to crime detention and prosecution. The CO may have come across an instance of harm thorough an initial s 7 visit or later either an interview and/or a medical examination. The police may then pursue this inquiry jointly or separately.

(2) Where the adult's consent cannot be obtained, the adult should be later informed about the use of this section.

(3) If the adult lacks the mental capacity to consent or is incapable of consenting because of difficulties with communication then the adult's proxy under the AWI Act should be approached to consent on his behalf. If the proxy refuses consent or is unavailable or unwilling to consent, then this power should still be used.

Where the proxy is a guardian under the AWI Act, it may be prudent for a CO to seek the views, and possible assistance, of the proxy's supervisor under the local authority duty to supervise a welfare guardian under AWI Act, s 10(1)(a). The supervisor would be a council employee within the same department. Similarly, the OPG also has to supervise guardians with either financial or property powers. In terms of a continuing power of attorney, intromission of funds and intervention orders, the OPG can also act on a complaint using s 6(2)(c) of the AWI Act. These powers alone may persuade the proxy to consent.

Office-holders from health, finance or other agencies linked to the adult have to consider the adult's right to confidentiality in relation to disclosing that information by looking to their

---

[13] Code of Practice, Chapter 8, paras 2, 4 and 15.

own Code of Practice for guidance. The Act's Code of Practice, however, states that "confidentiality is not an absolute right". Co-operation should be seen in the light of the objectives of the council's inquiry. Information too should be shared only on a "need to know" basis.[14]

Where adult consent is not obtained, it is good practice to inform the adult about any information sharing, unless a criminal inquiry is involved where crime detection and prosecution, as well as prevention, may provide legitimate grounds for disclosure. Safeguards in accessing and sharing information are linked to the principles of benefit, regard to the adult's past or present wishes and progressing matters with the adult's participation. Where relevant, the views of the adult's primary carer, guardian or attorney should be sought (s 2(b) and (c)).

The Act allows any records to be inspected by either the CO or a delegated person with, say, specialist knowledge of that type of record, for example an accountant (s 10(4)). Health records, on the other hand, may be inspected only by health professionals, probably in the form of a summary relating to past and current medical history linked to the specific nature of the harm to the patient (s 10(5)). "Health records" are defined as those relating to an individual's physical or mental health, made by any health professional caring for the individual (s 10(7)).

An agency can refuse access to records only if it can provide a "reasonable excuse" for refusing or otherwise failing to disclose as a written record. The Act specifically permits the council the option to have that person charged with obstruction using s 49(2). APCs may have inter-agency protocols to guide their councils on how to use the obstruction power where information is refused.

In Ina's case, it may be that the CO has to access bank accounts to help Ina to come to an arrangement to pay her council tax arrears in increments. If Ina has the capacity to permit this disclosure then consent would be in writing. If not, then Pt 2 of the Act could be used to establish what bank accounts Ina had in the first place and also the amount in each account.[15]

---

[14] Code of Practice, Chapter 8, para 8
[15] The Act, Pt 2, s 58 (s 24C of the AWI Act). The procedure for making such inquiries is discussed in Chapter 8.

3 ASSESSMENT ORDERS

An assessment order is one of three protection orders in the Act which are granted by a sheriff court. It is a legal means of taking an adult suspected of being seriously harmed from the place where they are visited, to be interviewed and /or medically examined in private. The criterion for these orders changes to that of "serious" harm, suggesting a higher level of risk compared with the investigation level. The sheriff grants the order on application by a council. It can be used for up to 7 days, presumably to allow for different kinds of assessments, and cannot be appealed. This is in contrast to a removal order the specific purpose of which is to prevent further harm to an adult at risk.

The issues of consent, undue pressure and incapacity also apply to this type of order. They are discussed along with the concepts of "adult at risk" and "harm" in Chapter 1. The following aspects of an assessment order are discussed:

- Definition
- Court criteria
- Application procedure

and the concept is illustrated by a case study at the end of this chapter.

DEFINITION

11 Assessment orders

(1) A council may apply to the sheriff for an order ("an assessment order") which authorises a council officer to take a specified person from a place being visited under section 7 in order to allow—

(a) a council officer, or any council nominee, to interview the specified person in private, and

(b) a health professional nominated by the council to conduct a private medical examination of the specified person,

for the purposes set out in subsection (2).

(2) Those purposes are to enable or assist the council to decide—

(a) whether the person is an adult at risk, and

(b) if it decides that the person is an adult at risk, whether it needs to do anything (by performing functions under this Part or otherwise) in order to protect the person from harm.

An assessment order is a protection order granted by a sheriff to allow a CO to take any adult from their place of being visited to another specified place, to be interviewed either by the CO or by a council nominee and/or to undergo a medical examination by a health professional. The purpose of these interviews would be to determine, first, whether the adult is an "adult at risk" and, second, whether the adult needs any support or protection from "harm". The term "adult at risk" is defined in s 3 and "harm" is defined in s 53 in this Act.

The evidence for this order may have come from a preliminary inquiry under s 4 of the Act, followed by a visit to the adult's place using the s 7 duties to visit and investigate what action is needed to protect the adult. However, these stages can be bypassed, depending on the adult's circumstances. The assessment order may be the only legal means of access to the adult until more evidence is available to prevent further harm.[1]

An assessment order lasts for 7 days after the sheriff grants the order. How the 7-day period is used will vary across Scotland, depending on the location of the specified place. It may be, for example, that in remote areas the adult could stay overnight at the place of assessment if travelling back the same day would not be feasible.

If harm is already established, the council could then consider a court action for either a removal order or a banning order under this Act or for other parallel legislation such as a guardianship order using the AWI Act.[2] The general principles of least restriction and of benefit would therefore have to be balanced by practicalities.

The point of the order is to afford the adult privacy and the opportunity to respond better to an interview or medical examination without being potentially subject to undue distress or duress by having it conducted in a place where harm is suspected. The timescales would determine how best this could be achieved.[3]

The adult cannot be detained for an interview or a medical examination against his will. The criteria therefore include the term "suitability" of a place for this purpose. The adult should

---

[1] Code of Practice, Chapter 9, para 3.
[2] See Chapter 9 for a discussion on the links with and differences from parallel legislation.
[3] Code of Practice, Chapter 9, para 9.

participate in this decision and say what is or is not suitable. This may then overcome the issue of a possible refusal to be interviewed or medically examined (s 2(d)) (participation principle: s 12(c)). The council may wish to seek other specified places in the order, given that the purpose of the assessment also includes a medical examination. An initial medical examination may lead to the need for a hospital assessment. The wording for this scenario in the application could therefore be "and to other places determined by the initial assessment", eg care home or day hospital.[4]

The court has to be satisfied that the applicant has considered the guiding principles around the adult's past and present wishes and the adult's participation. The key focus should be on carrying out an extensive assessment, having already argued the case for a suspicion of serious harm (s 3(2); s 12(a)). The assessment order also allows a CO a right to assess the adult in his current place of residence if this has a bearing on the type of harm suspected. This could be, for example, hazardous living conditions or inappropriate care by providers or health professionals in a care home, or even in a hospital.

The use of the assessment order applies equally where financial harm is suspected by contacting any financial agencies/companies linked to the adult. The adult's consent would be required or otherwise. If financial harm is suspected and the adult lacks capacity to consent, consideration should be given to using Pt 2 of the Act where a local authority now has powers to inquire from banks: see Chapter 7.

COURT CRITERIA FOR AN ASSESSMENT ORDER

12 Criteria for granting assessment order

The sheriff may grant an assessment order **only if satisfied—**
  (a) that the council has **reasonable cause** to **suspect** that the person in respect of whom the order is sought is an adult at risk who is **being, or is likely to be, seriously harmed,**
  (b) that the assessment order is required in order to establish whether the person is an adult at risk who is being, or is likely to be, seriously harmed, and
  (c) as to the **availability and suitability** of the place at which the person is to be interviewed and examined.

---

[4] This is speculation on the author's part and would need to be tested in court.

Significance of wording

- **only if satisfied**: this would be an individual judgement by each sheriff;
- **reasonable cause**: given that this is a civil action, the level of proof required is on the balance of probabilities;
- **suspect**: the council does not have to prove harm at this stage. Its suspicions will be largely based on the outcome of the visit using s 7 and also contact;
- **being, or is likely to be**: these are separate tests requiring separate evidence. In the first test ("being"), the council should produce paper and/or oral evidence to support the suspicion that the harm is happening. The second test ("likely to be") will rely more on professional judgement about the influences in the person's life that may lead to harm;
- **seriously harmed**: the term "seriously" will ultimately be decided in court. The interpretation of this will also depend on the type and extent of harm to the adult at risk. This could range from medical examination of injury to financial statements from institutions and sundry accounts such as fuel and credit cards;
- **availability and suitability**: the council should state where the adult would be taken using the order, in some cases along with written evidence of suitability. This could be more important if, for example, the place were a friend's house as opposed to a local authority resource.[5]

APPLICATION PROCEDURE: s 11(1)

An application is made through the sheriff court for the place where the adult lives. There are no standard forms, given that this is a summary application in terms of the civil law.[6] Only a council can apply. Application will be through the council legal services department. The council solicitors would use evidence from professionals who have already visited the adult under s 7.[7] Section 41(3) states that the council must notify the adult of the court application before lodging it. This notification must be done in writing.[8] It may also include a copy of the application itself. The sheriff must then "invite" the adult to be heard or represented

---

[5] Code of Practice, Chapter 9, paras 17 and 19 which suggest the need to evidence the least restrictive strategy in carrying out this order.

[6] See Chapter 7 for suggested court evidence for protection orders.

[7] Note that it is the council which applies and not a council officer. The officer may be a witness for the council if a s 7 visit was not successful.

[8] See Appendix 2 for a list of letters and a template information sheet to send to an adult.

before granting an assessment order (s 41(4)). A friend, a relative or any representative chosen by the adult can accompany him in court. This would be for support only, as opposed to giving evidence, although any party may also cite that person as a witness (s 41(5)). The use of the Vulnerable Witnesses (Scotland) Act 2004 ("VW Act") could be a consideration here.[9]

The sheriff can disapply any or all of the five standard court procedures listed in s 41(3)–(7) as follows:

- s 41(3) – notice by the council to the adult of the application;
- s 41(4) – notice from the sheriff to the adult of their right to be heard or to be legally represented in court;
- s 41(5) – the adult's right to be accompanied by a friend or relative or any other representative in court to support the adult only;
- s 41(6) – sheriff's right to appoint a safeguarder to safeguard the adult's interests;
- s 41(6) and (7) – appoint a safeguarder for any other purpose.

Before all or any of these rights are waived, the council has to satisfy the sheriff that doing so will protect the adult from serious harm or would not affect the legal rights of other people involved in the application. The council may therefore have to give separate evidence to allow the sheriff to dispense with each right. A blanket request to dispense with all of the five procedures (s 41(2)) should be used only under exceptional circumstances.

The sheriff also has discretion to appoint a safeguarder before deciding on the order. The safeguarder may, for example, be instructed to report on the issue of undue pressure. The adult may choose to make this request in order to challenge the council's evidence of, say, undue pressure or definition of "adult at risk" or "harm" (s 41(4)).

The sheriff must automatically attach a warrant to assist the CO in implementing any aspect of the assessment order. This warrant then allows the police to become involved. The Act uses the term "constable", reinforcing the general principle of least restriction and of benefit for the adult (who may be very alarmed at this point). The decision about use of police staff would depend too on the level of risk to the adult or any party involved at the place of removal.

The Act also states that a constable may use "reasonable force to fulfil the object of the visit". This is wider than the power to open lockfast places. It could, for example, mean anything from giving the adult a guiding hand to leave the premises to ensuring

---

[9] See Appendix 3 for information on applying these measures.

that another person does not stop the adult from leaving. The Act leaves it to the constable to decide what is reasonable.[10] It is the authority of the assessment order itself, however, that allows the CO to take the adult to a specified place, with or without police assistance.

The adult may or may not consent to the granting of the assessment order but then later refuse to consent to all or any of the actions in the order that include being interviewed and/ or medically examined. The Act recognises this right of refusal regardless of any court decision to overrule consent. Given that the purpose of the order is to remove the adult from the source of undue pressure, it is hoped that the adult's consent will be more readily given (s 8(3)).

CASE STUDY: MAY

May, aged 67, is widowed and lives alone. She has chronic heart disease and neglects her well-being by not heating her flat properly and paying poor attention to diet. As a result, she often becomes unwell and retires to bed for days on end. She has an only child, Colin. In the past, May did her shopping, housework and collected her own pension. Colin has gradually taken over these tasks now that his mother will not leave her house and spends most of her time in bed. Colin visits only to hand in food and her state pension. Colin resents his mother's growing dependence and thinks she should be making more of an effort.

A concerned neighbour refers May to the local council. She often hears raised voices between May and Colin. On one occasion, she overheard Colin saying "You would be better off dead". This neighbour is May's only social contact. May trusts and confides in her about Colin's lack of interest. May is not aware of the referral, as the neighbour knows she would be afraid of the consequences.

Application of assessment order

This case study follows the reasons for the council applying for an assessment order under the inquiry and investigation duties in the Act.

Neither May nor Colin is known to the social services department. May's GP has not seen her for over a year but

---

[10] See Chapter 7 for details on warrants.

confirmed a chronic heart complaint. Medical notes indicate a history of poor compliance with medication. The referring neighbour states that Colin lives nearby. Information at this s 4 inquiry stage without seeing May is therefore scant. There is, however, sufficient information to suggest that an investigation visit would be appropriate to establish whether anything needs to be done in order to protect May from harm by using a s 7 visit.

Prior to the visit, a CO writes to May about a date for a visit, stating the reasons for the visit under s 7 of the Act. The neighbour has given permission to disclose her name. The CO uses the supplementary provisions in the Act to bring with her a co-worker to record the visit.[11] Colin is present at this visit. May is in bed in a separate room upstairs. Colin follows the visitors to May's bedroom. May says very little. Her body language suggests an element of fear, especially when Colin raises his voice to the CO. Colin answers for May all the time. May remains silent and does not attempt to answer for herself. The CO exercises her powers under the supplementary provisions in the Act to see May's kitchen and inspect the cupboards and fridge. There is little food in both places. The house too seems neglected and the kitchen unclean.[12]

The CO tries to interview Colin using her powers under s 8, first by informing him of his right not to answer any or all of the questions.[13] Colin's only response is that his mother just wants to "curl up and die". Colin seems to be unaware of the extent of his mother's self-neglect. Colin blocks any follow-up arrangement to see May alone.

Discussion from this visit

In this case study, the evidence suggests that May could be an "adult at risk", using the s 3 criteria where she seems to be neglecting her health by not seeking medical treatment.

---

[11] Section 36(3)(b)(i). See Appendix 2 for template information to adapt in writing this letter.

[12] Section 36(3)(a) ("to examine the place"). This is a statutory power. If Colin refused this request, the council officer could apply to the court for a warrant under s 38(2).

[13] Section 8(1) and (2). If Colin had not been present in his mother's house the council officer would have had no legal right to interview, as any person eligible for an interview has to be present in the same place as the adult. Colin was notified in advance of the interview and chose to be present.

She has a physical illness (the chronic heart complaint) and her GP has confirmed that this will shorten her life if not treated. There seems to be an intimidating relationship between May and her son that suggests ongoing psychological harm

The s 4 inquiry tests for harm are "knows or believes". At this stage, there is a mixture of evidence. Colin is preventing the CO from interviewing his mother in private. The CO therefore has to produce evidence for the court to accept why an interview away from May's home would be beneficial and least restrictive. This would then allow for a more detailed discussion to explore with May the nature of any harm from Colin.

The CO discusses the findings of her visit with her manager. They follow council procedures and hold an adult protection case conference. May's GP sends a practice nurse with May's medical notes. A council solicitor also attends. The CO writes separately to May and Colin, inviting them to the case conference and also making them aware that a health professional will be present to discuss health issues. Neither party chooses to attend. May's neighbour is not invited, given the confidentiality of the information discussed. However, her referral is included in the initial report prepared by the CO.

At the conference, the practice nurse summarises May's medical notes that suggest lack of compliance and a history of depression because of her chronic illness.[14] The evidence recorded by the CO's co-worker is discussed in relation to assessing whether May is an adult at risk and is being subjected to serious harm. The council solicitor suggests that there is sufficient evidence to argue for an assessment order using the legal test in s 12.

Court application

The council solicitor makes an application to the sheriff court for the place where May lives, for an assessment order. The purpose of the application is to interview May and have her medically examined by her GP at the health centre. May is formally notified by the council and also by the sheriff clerk inviting them to attend court.

---

[14] The discussion of this information by the practice nurse could be viewed as a s 10 examination of records.

Colin has no right to be notified by the sheriff clerk under s 41(4) as he is not the subject of the application. Had May attended the court accompanied by her son for support under s 41(5), the council solicitor could have considered applying for the measures in the VW Act.[15] However, the sheriff can appoint a safeguarder who would then be entitled to contact Colin (s 41(6)).

Before the court date the CO visits May along with the co-worker from the first visit, to explain the application. This time, May is alone. She is apprehensive and fearful about the reaction from her son Colin, stating her fears that he will stop visiting and blame her for being mixed up with the court. May too thinks the letter from the sheriff clerk means that she has committed a crime. For these reasons she does not want to give the CO consent to the application.

From this visit, the CO decides that there is sufficient evidence to request that the sheriff waive May's consent to the application on the ground of undue pressure from Colin.[16] Colin phones the CO, expressing anger at all the fuss being created.

The sheriff hears evidence led by the council solicitor. The council witnesses are the CO, the co-worker and May's GP. There is also a written statement from May's neighbour who made the initial referral to the council. The GP states that May has capacity to decide against treatment and that he is aware of her having a poor prognosis for chronic heart disease. He confirms too that May has a history of poor compliance. The neighbour writes about May's account of constant friction between herself and Colin and gives that as a reason for neglecting herself.

The council argues for the assessment order to establish whether May is an "adult at risk" and is likely to be seriously harmed. It argues further for May's consent to be ignored because of the "undue pressure" from Colin, using the neighbour's evidence and also what May's co-worker recorded at the s 7 visit (s 11(2); s 35(3)).

Sheriff's decision – two scenarios

Scenario 1

The sheriff grants an assessment order without May's consent and orders that further investigations be made using

---

[15] Code of Practice, Chapter 9, para 29.
[16] Section 35(3).

the powers in s 8 and s 9. It is agreed that May's neighbour will accompany May to the health centre for this purpose.

The assessment order is used at the health centre for a morning-only assessment. May's neighbour accompanies her for support. This relaxes May who then agrees to an examination to monitor her heart and also to take blood tests. May's GP later prescribes medication for her heart disease and for depression. May allows her health to be monitored by regular visits from a health visitor who reports back to the GP.

The CO assesses May alone in the health centre, using the interview powers in s 8. May agrees to a care package for shopping and cooking, involving the home care department. May sees this as relieving the responsibility of her son. Through time, Colin eventually recognises the positive changes in his mother's health. Her mood lifts and she responds well to regular visits from her home help.

Scenario 2
The sheriff does not grant the assessment order, as there is insufficient evidence to suggest that May fulfils the "serious" harm or "adult at risk" tests using ss 3 and 12 respectively. The sheriff disagrees with the council's evidence of "undue pressure" from Colin towards his mother not to consent to the application. The sheriff believes that the evidence shows that Colin has consistently attempted in past years to encourage his mother to look after herself better but he has now given up. In short, the sheriff views Colin's recent behaviour as that of an exasperated son.

The sheriff does not think that moving May would be the least restrictive option and, moreover, it is likely that May would not answer questions or agree to a medical examination. The sheriff denies an oral request by the council solicitor to appoint a safeguarder, using his powers in s 41(6), without giving any reasons.

The council offers May a "life line" in terms of regular visits from a community care worker not related to the application. May reluctantly agrees, as both she and Colin now want to put the whole court business behind them.

One month later, Colin denies access to the community care worker when he is present. May does not answer the door when Colin is not there. The CO steps in and contacts

May's neighbour who confirms that the rowing between Colin and May had lessened immediately after the court case but they were back to their previous state. May's GP has visited twice and left a prescription but May's non-compliance has been the same as before.

The allocated CO therefore decides to make a second formal s 7 visit, this time with her manager as a witness. Access is denied. An adult protection case conference is convened, involving the same professionals as before. An assessment order is applied for, for a second time, within 2 months of the original application. Another sheriff hears the evidence and grants an assessment order.

4 REMOVAL ORDERS

A removal order is one of three protection orders created by the Act. It is a legal means of taking an adult suspected of being harmed from any place in Scotland to a specified place to protect him from harm. The sheriff court, on application by a council, grants the order. It can last for up to 7 days or less and cannot be appealed. The issues of consent, undue pressure and incapacity also apply to this order. They are discussed alongside the terms "adult at risk" and "harm" in Chapter 1. The components of a removal order are discussed under the headings below and illustrated with a case study at the end of the chapter:

- Definition
- Criteria for a removal order
- Application procedure
- Moving the adult at risk
- Safeguarding the adult's property during the removal order
- Variation or recall of a removal order.

DEFINITION: s 14

This is a protection order granted by a sheriff, allowing a CO to move any person who is over 16 years of age and likely to be seriously harmed to a specified place to protect them from further harm. The main focus is on removing the harmed person and not for assessment as understood in an assessment order. A removal order can be granted for up to 7 days from the day after it has been granted. However, the sheriff can grant a shorter time (s 14(2)). A removal order may facilitate other legal actions in the Act or parallel legislation.[1]

The evidence for this removal order would come from inquiries using the s 7 right to visit. Further evidence may also be available from an assessment order if the adult could not be interviewed

---

[1] The integration of this and other legislation is a starting point in the Act under s 7(1) that states "whether it needs to do anything (by performing functions under this Part or otherwise)".

safely in his own place. The evidence would be on the risk to the adult and not their response to the assessment order.

A removal order may, on the other hand, be the only legal means of protection until more evidence is available to prevent further harm. In a positive sense, it could be interpreted as a "breathing space" between the specified person and the alleged harmer. This approach should be argued in court as opposed to detaining an adult (see questions from professionals below with regard to an adult with incapacity).

CRITERIA FOR A REMOVAL ORDER

15 *Criteria for granting removal order*

(1) The sheriff may grant a removal order only if **satisfied**—
   (a) that the person in respect of whom the order is sought is an adult at risk who is **likely** *to be* **seriously harmed** *if not moved to another place, and*
   (b) as to the **availability and suitability** *of the* **place** *to which the adult at risk is to be moved.*

Significance of wording

- **satisfied**: the sheriff's interpretation of the evidence;[2]
- **likely**: the legal test is based on a civil application to describe the actions or possible actions of the harmer. Even at this stage, the suspected harmer may not yet have actually harmed the adult at risk, so a removal order can be used to protect the adult from this possibility;
- **seriously harmed**: this is a qualification of the legal definition of "harm" in s 52(1). The seriousness of the harm will therefore relate to how it affects the adult. Evidence would be specific to the type of harm, eg physical (medical; psychological); eyewitnesses (recording what the harmed adult says); property, rights or interests (evidence from banks, credit card companies and so forth). Given that this is a civil action, the legal test is one on the balance of probabilities;
- **availability and suitability**: the council should obtain a written agreement from the owner of a specified place if this were, say, a private home to confirm the owner's willingness to receive the adult for up to 7 days. The applicant would also have to prove suitability;

---

[2] See Chapter 7 for guidance on evidence.

- **place**: there will probably be one specific place for the adult to stay for the duration of the order. However, there may be a need for more flexibility in the social care plan to allow for visits to other locations.

The council has to prove that:

- the adult is an "adult at risk" as defined in s 3 of the Act;
- the adult is likely to be seriously harmed if not moved to another place;
- a suitable place is available to which to remove the adult.

These three conditions are for the adult's physical safety. The risk element is defined in s 3 of the Act:

- unable to safeguard their own well-being, property, rights or other interests;
- at risk of harm (defined later in the Act under s 52 – actions by others and also self-harm);
- more vulnerable to harm than other people not affected by disability, mental disorder, illness or physical or mental infirmity.

The legal test is the sheriff's "satisfaction". Given that the removal order application is a civil one, the level of proof required is on the balance of probabilities. The evidence will be tested in court, regardless of the source and also in the light of the adult's consent (or refusal to consent if this is the case). The sheriff has to consider how the removal order will be least restrictive and also beneficial according to the general principles in the Act.

If the adult is capable of giving informed consent but refuses to do so and this is known prior to the granting of the order (as s 35 is based on the premise of known refusal), the applicant has to prove that there is undue pressure against the adult to refuse consent.

The evidence to assess "serious harm" may already have been placed before the court in an assessment order. If not, the same evidence would be used because of a visit under s 4, or additional evidence gained from use of an assessment order. The sheriff must also be satisfied that a specified place is available and suitable for the adult to be moved to.

APPLICATION PROCEDURE: s 14(1)(b)

The procedure is the same for an assessment order where an application is made to the sheriff court for the place where the adult lives. There are no standard forms, given that this is a summary application in terms of the civil law.[3] Only a council can apply. This will be through a council solicitor using evidence from professionals who have already visited the adult under a s 7 visit.[4]

Section 41(3) states that the council must notify the adult of the court application before lodging it. This must be done in writing. The sheriff must "invite" the adult to be heard or represented before granting an assessment order. This invitation should state the adult's right to be heard and to be legally assisted (s 41(4)). The court also allows the adult to be accompanied by a friend, a relative or any representative ot their choice to support them in court. This would be for support only, as opposed to giving evidence, although any party may also cite that person as a witness (s 41(5)). The use of measures in the VW Act could be a consideration if the adult is giving evidence. See Appendix 3 for a discussion on how to apply for these measures.

The sheriff can disapply any or all of the five standard court procedures listed in s 41(3)–(7) as follows:

- s 41(3) – notice by the council to the adult of the application;
- s 41(4) – an invitation from the sheriff to the adult of their right to be heard or to be legally represented in court;
- s 41(5) – the adult's right to be accompanied by a friend or relative or any other representative in court to support the adult only;
- s 41(6) – sheriff's right to appoint a safeguarder to safeguard the adult's interests;
- s 41(6 and 7) – appoint a safeguarder for any other purpose.

The additional court procedure that can be waived in a removal order is s 15(3) (legal representation for the adult and others listed), where conditions are to be attached to the removal order.

Before all or any of these six procedures are waived, the council has to satisfy the sheriff that doing so will protect the adult from serious harm or would not affect the legal rights of other people involved in the application. The council may therefore have to give separate evidence to allow the sheriff to dispense with each right. A blanket request to dispense with all six procedures should be used only under exceptional circumstances (s 41(2)(a) and (b)).

The sheriff can attach conditions to the removal order. The purpose of these conditions or requirements would be to allow

---

[3] See Chapter 7 for suggested court evidence for protection orders.
[4] Note that it is the council which applies and not a council officer. The officer may be a witness for the council following a s 7 visit.

contact between the adult and the harmer under supervised conditions as a first step to resolving the reason for the harm (s 15(2)). The conditions for contact could be outlined in an access plan. This would include dates/times and perhaps another location. This comes under the term "specified conditions" in s 15(2)(b).[5] Other conditions may be that specified people are family or friends, or even another professional to care or treat the affected adult.

There is no right of appeal (s 51(1)). There is no formal notification process to the adult after the removal order is granted. Section 16 states that the order is in itself sufficient authority to take the adult to a specified place. These details will be recorded in the removal order.

Should access to implement a removal order be denied then a "warrant to enter" is required to allow a constable to assist the CO in carrying out any powers in the removal order. The warrant is automatically granted on request when the order is granted (s 39(1)).[6] If the adult is moved to another place within the sheriffdom of the court, the order can still be used. If the adult is moved to a separate part of Scotland outwith the first court's jurisdiction, then a fresh application would have to be made to the nearest court to where the adult has been taken.

A removal order can be varied any number of times within the period of the order. This is probably unlikely, given the court process involved. An application to recall or vary the removal order can be made only by:

- the adult;
- any person with an interest in the adult's well-being or property;
- the council (s 17(4)).

A sheriff can recall or vary a removal order if satisfied that there has been a change in the "facts or circumstances" from the time the order was granted or varied (s 17(1)). If the removal order is recalled, the sheriff can direct the council to return the adult to his original place or to a place of his choice. The place of choice would be recorded in the sheriff's direction under s 17(3)(b) and should be within the council's capacity to carry out.[7]

---

[5] Providing a plan in the application is not a legal requirement, as for the two powers in a banning order. It may be an easier means to explain to the court any request to consider s 15(2).

[6] See Chapter 7 for a discussion on warrants.

[7] A CO need not necessarily return the adult. This could be done by a person known to the adult.

MOVING THE ADULT AT RISK: s 16

The key focus in a removal order is to prevent the likelihood of serious harm to a person who has been proved to be an "adult at risk". The place where the adult actually lives may, however, be a contributory factor in the harm. The adult must be removed to a "specified place", which has been assessed as both "available and suitable" for the purpose (s 15(1)(b)). The adult cannot be detained in this place and can therefore leave at will. The test for "suitability" should take into account the adult's wishes in the application, to offer maximum benefit during the period of removal.

The maximum removal period is 7 calendar days, not including the day the sheriff signs the order. The order would expire at midnight on the last day. The moved person cannot be returned home and removed again within this period. The expiry date can therefore be set at any time within that period. Although the court has powers to grant a maximum of 7 days in a removal order, the council should always argue for shorter periods, in line with the general principles of benefit, least restriction and, most importantly, the moved person's wishes.

The Act allows the CO to arrange for the removal to be planned for up to 72 hours before the removal order starts. This will vary for each case, given the diversity of circumstances open to any council in Scotland. This 72-hour period will allow time for planning and negotiation with the moved person and with other parties involved. The removal order itself allows the CO to enter any place to remove an adult. This includes the right to enter any adjacent place to access the adult. This could be, for example, in a private lodgings location or on board a ship harboured alongside other boats (s 16). There is no specified place in a removal order from which an adult can be removed, compared with an assessment order. This means that "place" can be wherever the adult happens to be after the order is granted. It may, for example, be that the adult is being moved by the harmer in order to avoid the consequences of the removal order.[8]

The court will record on the removal order where the specified place is. Good practice would suggest that the council would include removal details, perhaps in the form of a strategic "access plan" to follow through the actual removal itself.[9]

Although the Act does not detail what should happen after the removal order expires, the council continues to have a duty

---

[8] A sheriff may, however, decide to include in the removal order that the adult can be removed only from a specified place.

[9] Code of Practice, Chapter 10, para 42.

of care to return the adult safely to his place. The Code of Practice suggests that the council prepare a "support plan" with the adult to progress the adult's care after the removal order expires or indeed if the adult wishes to leave at any time. This need not be in the application.[10]

If, after being returned, the adult continues to require protection, the council may have to consider using another protection order, a banning order, or the use of other legislation for legal support.

In the event of access being denied to the CO to implement a removal order or a varied removal order, a sheriff is required to grant a warrant for entry along with the order (s 39). This attached warrant allows a constable to assist in gaining entry to the barred premises and also to assist the CO in moving the person to the specified place stated in the removal order. The only difficulty is that the council has to record a specific place in the warrant. If the adult had no fixed abode then a warrant to enter a specified place under s 37(1)(a) could not be used. The police may be able to advise where this situation applies. It is the authority of the removal order itself and not the warrant that allows the adult to be moved from the premises. The purpose of the warrant is only to assist the CO to carry out the removal order (s 37(1)(b)).

SAFEGUARDING THE ADULT'S PROPERTY DURING THE REMOVAL ORDER: s 18

The council has a duty to protect the adult's property after he has been moved. This is detailed in s 18, which is in seven parts. The emphasis is on protecting the adult's property, whether "owned or controlled", from being lost or damaged. The main legal actions open to the council in relation to property are:

- to prevent it from being lost or damaged (s 18(1));
- to enter any place to remove the property (s 18(2));
- to take any reasonable steps to safeguard the property (s 18(4)).

The council cannot charge the adult for maintaining or storing his property (s 18(5)). The authority to supervise the adult's property ceases after the removal order expires (s 18(6)). The council then has to return the property to the adult: the Act states "as soon as is reasonably practicable". This could be discussed in advance with the adult in the form of an agreed plan (s 18(7)).

---

[10] Code of Practice, Chapter 10, para 59.

Property could be the contents of a house; a vehicle; animals (including livestock); cash; money in bank accounts; credit cards; and clothing. The controlling element of the council's duties could be to keep the property lockfast or, in the case of animals, in secure accommodation

VARIATION OR RECALL OF A REMOVAL ORDER: s 17

The Act allows the council, the adult or any person with an interest in the adult's well-being or property to apply to the same court to have the removal order varied or recalled. Given the maximum 7-day timescale of the order, this right may not be used often. The adult too has to consent to being subject to the removal order at any time the order is being implemented (s 35(2)). If consent has been waived because of undue pressure or lack of capacity, the council may use this section if, for example, the specified place is unsuitable and the adult should be moved to another place or the order recalled. The sheriff then has the discretion to direct that the adult be returned to his original place or to any another place (s 17(3)).[11]

CASE STUDY: JIMMY AND SARAH (HIS MOTHER)

Jimmy is a 65-year-old single man with mild cerebral palsy and learning disabilities. He lives with his widowed mother, Sarah, aged 93. Jimmy has two siblings but they live abroad. He and Sarah are isolated except for the private home help who visits four times per week to do housework and shopping.

The home help often witnesses arguments between Jimmy and his mother. On one occasion, she witnessed them fighting and had to intervene. When the situation calmed down, she discussed with them the most appropriate action to prevent more friction. She suggested contacting the local social services department. Both Jimmy and Sarah readily agreed to this plan.

A social worker visited by arrangement, with the private home help present. The information shared was very honest. The outcome was that the social worker would make regular monitoring visits to the house. The home help would continue with her work, on the understanding that the social worker and the home help would keep in contact.

---

[11] Code of Practice, Chapter 10, para 54.

The social worker also contacted Jimmy's siblings abroad who agreed to this plan.

Four months after the first incident, the social worker received a telephone call from the home help to say that Sarah had a small bruise on her face. She reported too that arguments between Jimmy and Sarah had started again a few days before this incident. The family GP visited but could not conclusively state the cause of the bruise, given Sarah's age and the likelihood of bruising from any slight injury. Both Jimmy and his mother would not discuss what happened and wanted to remain together.

Application for a removal order

The issue for the council is to decide who the adult at risk is, using the three-pronged criteria in s 3(1). Arguably, both Sarah and Jimmy fulfil the criteria in terms of not being able to safeguard their own well-being, the mutual psychological and, perhaps, physical harm caused through their arguments; and, finally, their medical conditions where Jimmy has a disability and Sarah is infirm, making them more vulnerable to being harmed.

The council has to apply the general principle tests in s 1 of least restriction and of benefit to either adult. Given that the care in the home is primarily for Sarah, the council decided it would be more restrictive to remove her from a familiar environment. The decision is taken to apply for a protection order to remove Jimmy in order to assess how Sarah copes on her own with the help of a carer and whether there is further injury in the home in Jimmy's absence. The positive argument for a removal order is to allow Jimmy and Sarah breathing space from each other.[12] If this removal order were to be effective, the council could plan regular breaks for either Jimmy or Sarah, with their agreement, to relieve the stress of their constant contact and to minimise further harm.

The council makes a court application for a removal order. Given the imminent nature of the possible harm, the council requests that the sheriff dispense with the court procedures under s 41(2)(a) and (b). The witnesses are the private home help, the CO and the family GP. All three

---

[12] Code of Practice, Chapter 10, para 2.

give evidence that Jimmy is an "adult at risk" under s 3, as follows:

- unable to safeguard his well-being and other interests: Jimmy is frustrated being alone with his mother and this has spilled over into violence;

- risk of harm: the rows with his mother cause Jimmy distress (Jimmy's home help has witnessed this);

- disability: the GP confirms Jimmy's cerebral palsy and mild learning disabilities.

Court decision

The CO contacts Jimmy's siblings who persuade him to consent to the order. Jimmy is reassured by their support and the fact they are not blaming him for what happened. Jimmy's mother is similarly reassured.

The sheriff disapplies the notification rights on the ground that there may be immediate danger of further harm (s 41(2)(a) and (b)).

The sheriff grants a removal order but only for 4 days to allow some "breathing space" between Jimmy and his mother. The sheriff specifies conditions of access to Jimmy's mother and to the private home help whom Jimmy trusts. Access by Jimmy's mother is initially by telephone and then one visit (s 15(2)(b)).

The council identifies a local care home as being available and suitable as a specified place (s 15(1)(b)).

Longer-term plans

Jimmy is taken to the care home, initially for 4 days. His mother's telephone calls and visit reassure Jimmy that he has not been abandoned. The CO chooses to use this time apart to suggest further regular breaks such as day care and separate respite care for Jimmy. A long-term care plan along these lines is prepared before Jimmy is taken back to his mother. These agreements are set up on a voluntary basis.

The purpose of the removal order was to prevent further harm, but at the same time to build in long-term support to keep Jimmy and his mother safely together. In other words, a long-term harm-reduction strategy is necessary to prevent repetition.

QUESTION FROM PROFESSIONALS[13]

1. Is an adult, who lacks capacity and is made subject to a removal order, not "detained"? The letter of the law says no – but how can someone in such a position take the decision to leave? The court can appoint a curator *ad litem* but, realistically, can a curator make representations to a court within the 7 days of a removal order's duration?

RESPONSE

This is a fair point. The sheriff has to consider any application for a protection order in terms of support and protection and not detention, although the effect on the adult is the same, ie removal without consent to prevent further serious harm. Both Acts have court notification and representation rights that will determine whether the order is granted. The Act too allows conditions to be attached to a removal order involving contact from specified persons that could include the person harming the adult.

The codes of practice in both Acts also stress the importance of using the removal period to maximum benefit and as a contingency plan to a longer-term solution to a more suitable environment for either care and treatment (2003 Act); or support and protection (the Act). In short, a removal order is an interim measure to this end. The longer-term plan could be part of the supporting evidence for a removal order.

VIEWS OF SERVICE USERS AND CARERS[14]

Protection orders (ss 11, 14 and 19):

- could help with domestic abuse cases – "I called for help from the police and they said they couldn't do anything as it was classed as a domestic";
- disabled people rate their quality of life higher than professionals do, including sheriffs;

---

[13] This is from a selection of questions raised by professionals training sessions for the Act. They came from Ian Kinsley, Care Training Matters Ltd. The phraseology is intact. The response above is from this author.

[14] This is a selection of concerns expressed in relation to different functions of the Act, discussed at a conference for service users and carers called "What It Means to Me" held by the Scottish Government on 21 August 2008.

- concerns about the experience, background and training safeguarders have in disabled people's values;
- removal orders could be used as a "back door" to put people into nursing homes;
- families could be split up: "A banning order could remove the most important people in the adult's life."

5   BANNING ORDERS

A banning order is one of the three protection orders in the Act granted by a sheriff to protect an adult ("adult at risk") who has been harmed by a person ("the subject") within Scotland. The banning order can last for up to 6 months. Also available is a selection of attached conditions either to bring the adult and the subject together to resolve the harm or to reinforce the need to keep them apart (s 19(1) and (2)).

The sheriff can also grant a temporary banning order on an emergency basis pending this application, with the same powers available as for a banning order (s 21).

If several subjects are involved in harming the same adult, then separate banning orders would be required, as each subject can challenge the application and, where appropriate, have different conditions attached to their order.

The applicant can be the adult or any person entitled to occupy the place where the adult is. The council has a default duty to apply for a banning order; this default duty is qualified in s 22(2) of the Act which is similar to the AWI Act in relation to intervention and guardianship orders. In other words, both Acts open these powers to the public. The council has a duty to apply only as a last resort.

The issues of consent, undue pressure and incapacity also apply to banning orders. They are discussed in Chapter 1 along with the terms "adult at risk" and "harm". The components of a banning order are discussed below and illustrated with a case study.

This chapter is necessarily longer than the two previous ones, given the range of options and practice procedures available. Where possible, therefore, the Code of Practice will be referred to for information.

- Banning orders – definition
- Temporary banning orders
- Criteria for a banning order
- Application procedure
- Variation or recall of banning order
- Breaching a full or temporary banning order and power of arrest.

BANNING ORDERS – DEFINITION

19 Banning orders

*(1) A banning order is an order granted by the sheriff which bans the subject of the Order ("the **subject**") from being in a **specified place**.*

(2) A banning order may also—

*(a) ban the subject from being in a **specified area** in the **vicinity** of the **specified place**,*

*(b) authorise the **summary ejection** of the subject from the specified place and the specified area,*

(c) prohibit the subject from moving any specified thing from the specified place,

*(d) direct any **specified person** to take **specified measures** to preserve any **moveable property** owned or controlled by the subject which remains in the specified place while the order has effect,*

*(e) be made subject to any **specified conditions**;*

(f) require or authorise any person to do, or to refrain from doing, anything else that the sheriff thinks necessary for the proper enforcement of the order.

Significance of wording

- **subject**: this is a person of any age who is allegedly harming the adult at risk. Section 30(2) includes children who have the capacity to understand court proceedings;[1]
- **specified place**: this will be where the adult lives;
- **specified area**: this is the town, village or part of the city where the adult lives;[2]
- **vicinity**: this could be a specific street where the adult lives (including the adult's address, depending on local geography, ie a rural or urban setting);
- **summary ejection**: removing the subject from the adult's place when the subject refused to leave. This would be a police action;
- **specified person**: a council officer (CO), or council nominee;

---

[1] The Children (Scotland) Act 1995 sets out that a child can hold a view, exercise that view and have it taken into account (depending on their age and maturity) when they are 12 years old or above.

[2] The Act specifies a place where an adult is as "the area which the person is for the time being". This is explained within the definition of "council" in s 53 (Interpretation of Part 1).

- **specified measures**: these are ways to protect the subject's valuables, sanctioned by the sheriff;
- **moveable property**: examples – the subject's furniture, or a pet;
- **specified conditions**: a strategy to reconcile the adult with the subject in order to resolve the cause of the harm to the adult.[3]

A banning order is a court order under s 19(1) that allows a person of any age ("the subject") to be banned from being in a specific place where the adult lives. The main focus of the banning order is to protect the adult from any or further serious harm by the subject. A banning order can be used on its own, depending on the threat of harm to the adult. A CO using the s 7 investigation powers to gather evidence for such an application may have visited the adult.

The banning order can also attach a further six conditions under s 19(2)(a)–(f), listed below in order. The banning order can contain a mixture of these powers, with the paramount aim of protecting the adult from harm. The conditions are discussed in detail below to highlight their individual importance:

(a) The subject is banned from being in a specified area in the vicinity of the specified place. This could include, for example, a day care centre, a pub or the perimeter of where the adult lives, such as the street or district. The adult may have been abused or harassed when attending or living in such places. In short, this condition allows freedom of interpretation.

(b) Authorising the summary ejection of the subject from the specified area and place where the adult lives. This condition is twinned with (a) above. The subject could either be in the adult's place when the order is made or have returned there and now refuses to leave.

> *Example*: a son (the subject) visits his mother in a sheltered housing complex and creates a disturbance outside the complex. The mother (the adult) contacts the police to have her son ejected using this condition. The mother has immediate police protection. The son may then be charged with breach of the peace, with or without a power of arrest (see below).

If the applicant is seeking either of the first two conditions, they are required to submit a "plan" to identify the

---

[3] See Chapter 7 for suggested guidance on evidence for protection orders.

specified area in the application (see application procedure below).

(c) Stopping the subject from removing any specified thing from the adult's specified place. This could be a single condition attached to the banning order to prevent a subject moving something of value from the adult's place. If the item is then moved, the subject may be charged with theft.[4]

(d) Allowing a specified person to preserve any moveable property owned or controlled by the subject which is still in the adult's specified place.

The applicant should obtain an inventory of moveable property, signed by the subject. Unlike a removal order for the adult, the Act does not state whether the applicant for the banning order has to incur expenses for preserving the subject's property. This may be a factor in deciding whether or not this measure is attached.[5]

The subject can formally request this measure as part of his right to be heard by the sheriff before the application is determined (s 41(4)). If this condition is likely to be necessary, the applicant should not request a disapplication of the subject's right to be represented in s 41(2)(a). It follows that if the subject is not given this right, he could apply to the sheriff to vary the order using s 24 (see details on s 41(2) (disapplication of court procedure) below).

(e) The banning order can be subject to any specified conditions. This is clarified in s 19(3) to include supervision of the subject in the area or place banned. This may be to allow some form of mediation between the subject and the adult. Given that this is a summary application, the conditions should be tailored to suit individual circumstances. This approach is similar to guardianship orders using the AWI Act.

(f) These are the sheriff's discretionary powers to "require or authorise" any person to do, or refrain from doing, anything else to enforce the banning order. The suggestion may come from the applicant, a safeguarder or the sheriff himself in the course of the hearing. The use of this condition will vary on an individual basis. For example,

---

[4] In time, an application for this condition may be used widely by the adult or a person occupying the same place (s 22(1)). The optional power of arrest and the possibility of a police charge may be another attraction for the public to seek this in court (s 25; s 32(1)(b)).

[5] Code of Practice, Chapter 11, para 58.

it could be controlling the subject's access to people connected with the adult, such as family (see case study on Grace, below).

TEMPORARY BANNING ORDERS: s 21

This is an order that can be granted on an interim basis until the evidence is heard for a full banning order. It has to be lodged along with a banning order application.[6] It may have the same powers as a banning order but it is usually imposed for a shorter period than the maximum 6 months (s 21(2)).[7] The Sheriff Court Rules require the banning order application to be determined (decided) within a specific period that would be in the spirit of the "least restrictive" approach (s 21(3)). Similarly, a temporary banning order expires when a full banning order application hearing is determined (s 21(4)(a)).

A temporary banning order may be appropriate if the applicant is confident that there will be a resolution to the relationship between the affected adult and the subject of the order. The temporary banning order itself may be a source of evidence for the court to consider before granting a full banning order, ie proof that the order and/or the further conditions in s 19(1) and (2) were successful or indeed have failed. The measures in the temporary banning order may then be varied in the full banning order. The general and guiding principles in ss 1 and 2 should help in arguing for this need. A temporary banning order can be recalled at any time before the full banning order is determined (s 24(2)(b)).

CRITERIA FOR A BANNING ORDER: s 20

20 Criteria for granting banning order

The sheriff may grant a banning order only if satisfied—
  (a) *that an adult at risk is being, or is likely to be, seriously harmed by another person,*
  (b) *that the adult at risk's well-being or property would be better safeguarded by banning that other person from a place occupied by the adult than it would be by moving the adult from that place, and*

---

[6] Act of Sederunt (Summary Applications, Statutory Applications and Appeals etc Rules) 1999 (SI 1999/929), r 3.35.3(2), inserted by Act of Sederunt (Summary Applications, Statutory Applications and Appeals etc Rules) Amendment (Adult Support and Protection (Scotland) Act 2007) (No 2) 2008 (SSI 2008/335), para 2.

[7] SI 1999/929, r 3.35.3(3), inserted by SSI 2008/335, para 2.

    (c) that either—
        (i) the adult at risk is entitled, or permitted by a third
            party, or
        (ii) neither the adult at risk nor the subject is entitled, or
            permitted by a third party, to occupy the place from
            which the subject is to be banned.

The applicant has to produce evidence to prove that the adult is being, or is likely to be, seriously harmed by another person. The evidence to assess "serious harm" may already have been placed before the court in an application for an assessment order or possibly a removal order. If not, the same evidence would be used as a result of an investigation visit using s 7. See Chapter 1 for a discussion of the terms "adult at risk" and "harm".

The legal test is the sheriff's "satisfaction". The sheriff also has to consider that the banning order will be least restrictive and beneficial for the adult, according to the general principles in the Act. Section 20(b) terms this as "well-being or property would be better safeguarded". The interpretation of "well-being" should be linked to the key factors causing the adult to be harmed. The adult's property can range from his home or its contents to pets.

If the council is not the default applicant for the banning order it may be required to act as a witness for either the adult or any other person living with the adult. The reason for this is that only the council has the legal authority under the Act to investigate whether or not an adult is an "adult at risk" or is being seriously harmed. The council too can make further inquiries under s 5 to a list of public bodies, including financial companies, to prove "harm" as defined under s 53(1) above.

If the adult is capable of giving informed consent but refuses consent to the banning order, the applicant has to prove that there is "undue pressure" against the adult to refuse consent. This term is discussed in Chapter 1.

If occupancy rights belong solely to the subject of the order and not jointly with the adult, the subject cannot be banned from the place. Section 23 interprets occupancy rights by way of the Matrimonial Homes (Family Protection) (Scotland) Act 1981 ("MH Act") to ensure that the adult cannot ban someone entitled to occupancy where the adult is not so entitled. The MH Act was amended by the Civil Partnership Act 2004 to ensure that the MH Act applies to civil partners exactly as it does to married couples. The MH Act also applies to cohabiting heterosexual couples.[8]

---

[8] 2007 Act, s 23. Code of Practice, Chapter 11, paras 23–25. The council's legal services department should give specific advice on this complex issue of entitlement. The above is only an outline.

Given the maximum length of a banning order, the applicant must have strong evidence to argue for the full 6-month period. This is why s 19(5)(a) includes the restriction of a specified expiry date.

If the nature of the harm becomes a criminal matter involving a formal charge by the police, the applicant may wish to argue for a full-term banning order of 6 months, to allow the court to decide on the charge if the subject is not detained in custody. A civil banning order may therefore be the best means to protect the adult from further harm. It may also be that the subject has yet to be tried for the charges before the 6-month banning period expires. The applicant (more than likely the council) may wish to apply to the sheriff for another banning order to allow this charge to be dealt with through the court system. The evidence for doing so could be supported by the police and the procurator fiscal.[9]

APPLICATION PROCEDURE: s 22

22 Right to apply for a banning order

(1) An application for a banning order may be made **only by or on behalf of**—

   (a) an adult whose well-being or property would be safeguarded by the order,

   (b) any other person who is entitled to occupy the place concerned, or

   (c) where subsection (2) applies, the council.

(2) The council **must apply** for a banning order if it is satisfied—

   (a) as to the matters set out in **section 20**,

   (b) that **nobody else is likely to apply** for a banning order in respect of the circumstances which caused the council to be satisfied as to those matters, and

   (c) that **no other proceedings** (under this Part or otherwise) to eject or ban the person concerned from the place concerned are depending before a court.

Significance of wording

- **only by or on behalf of**: this means any party or his solicitor;
- **adult**: this means the "adult at risk" as defined in s 3;
- **must apply**: this is a mandatory default duty for the council;

---

[9] This is discussed in the Code of Practice, Chapter 11, paras 77 and 78.

- **section 20**: this refers to the section in the Act entitled "Criteria for granting banning order";
- **nobody else is likely to apply**: the council should be able to prove this by formal consent from the adult, where applicable;
- **no other proceedings**: the council should check with the sheriff clerk whether another person has lodged a banning order.

The adult or anyone entitled to live in the same premises may apply for a banning order. The term "entitled" refers to occupancy rights. Examples of joint occupancy rights could be the same lodgings, a joint tenancy, and joint mortgages with the adult. These rights should be proved in court. This section applies where the source of the harm affects both the adult and the other person living with the adult. The terms "well-being" and "property" in the application criteria should apply mainly to the adult but also, by default, to the other person in the same place.

The Act allows an application by either party to be lodged by a representative, probably a solicitor under the legal aid scheme.[10]

Given that this is a summary application, there is no statutory form. Rule 3.35.3 of SI 1999/929 details the process of application. In summary, this is:

(i)   a "plan" must be lodged for condition s 19(2)(a) or (b);
(ii) a temporary banning order application must be lodged with a full application for a banning order;
(iii) where a temporary order is lodged, the full application must be heard within 6 months;
(iv) an application to vary or recall with a banning or temporary banning order must be made in the light of the original order.

The council, through its legal services department, has a default duty to apply for a banning order if no one else is likely to apply and it has evidence to support the application (s 22(1)(c)).

When considering an application to ban a child, a referral could be made to the Children's Reporter where it is believed that there would be an effective case to answer. In urgent circumstances a referral should be made at the same time as the application for an order. Section 30(2) applies only to cases when the police have already arrested a child under the power of arrest.[11]

---

[10] See the Legal Aid website for further information: http://www.slab.org.uk/publications/index.html. The emergency legal aid provisions still apply.
[11] Code of Practice, Chapter 11, para 15.

The Act states that the order should expire at the earliest of the following periods:

(a) any specified expiry date;
(b) the date of a recalled order;
(c) 6 months after it is granted (s 19(5)).

The applicant should argue for as short a period as possible in accordance with the general principles of the adult's wishes and what would be beneficial. Applicants may need some guidance from the council who may be involved in mediation to resolve the reasons for the harm as quickly as possible.

The applicant for the banning order must notify both the subject of the application and the adult of his court application, before lodging the application. This must be done in writing (s 41(3)). Also, the sheriff must "invite" the affected adult at risk and the subject of the application to be heard or represented by a solicitor before granting any protection order, which includes a banning order.[12] The adult can choose a friend, a relative or any representative, for example the adult's social worker, to accompany him in court (s 41(5)). The key term here is "accompany", as opposed to legally representing the adult under s 41(4). This could be linked with the measures available in the VW Act. See Appendix 3 for a discussion on how to use this legislation.

The sheriff can disapply any or all of the five standard court procedures listed in s 41(3)–(7) as follows:

- s 41(3): notice by the council to the adult regarding the application;
- s 41(4): an invitation from the sheriff to the adult on his right to be heard or to be legally represented in court;
- s 41(5): the adult's right to be accompanied by a friend or relative or any other representative in court, to support the adult only;
- s 41(6): sheriff's right to appoint a safeguarder to safeguard the adult's interests;
- s 41(6 and 7): appoint a safeguarder for any other purpose.

The additional court procedure that can be waived in a banning order is contained in s 19(4) – legal representation for the adult and others listed, where conditions are to be attached to bring the subject and the adult together during the period of the banning order.

---

[12] I am uncertain as to who should send a copy of the application – the applicant or the sheriff clerk.

Before all or any of these procedures are waived, the applicant has to satisfy the sheriff that doing so will protect the adult from serious harm or would not affect the legal rights of other people involved in the application. The applicant may therefore have to give separate evidence to allow the sheriff to dispense with each right. A blanket request to dispense with all six procedures should be used only under exceptional circumstances (s 41(2)(a) and (c)).

The subject's rights to apply to have moveable property in the adult's place would have to be included in the application where appropriate (s 19(2)(d)).

There is a right of appeal to the sheriff principal for the granting of, or the refusal to grant, a full banning order. The sheriff, however, has discretion to allow such an appeal from any party against a temporary banning order. The appeal periods are 14 and 7 days for a banning and temporary banning order respectively (s 51(2); SSI 2008/335). Where the sheriff principal grants an appeal the order is granted with no further appeal to the Court of Session. Where the sheriff principal quashes (cancels) an order that a sheriff has granted, the sheriff principal's decision can then be appealed to the Court of Session. The order originally granted by the sheriff, however, continues pending the decision of the Court of Session. Five appeal conditions are listed in s 51(4).[13]

After the banning order is granted, the applicant has to notify the adult or any other person with an interest in the imposition of the banning order. The notification is a copy of the banning order itself which the court will issue using standard court procedure forms. The Act states that a failure to notify will not invalidate the banning order but this should be standard practice in any case (s 26(4)).

VARIATION OR RECALL OF BANNING ORDER: s 24

Any party listed in s 24(3) can later apply to have a banning order or a temporary banning order varied or recalled using s 24(1). These parties now include the subject of the order; the original applicant for the order listed in s 22(1); the adult; or any other person who has an interest in the adult's well-being or property. Any party can apply to vary or recall as often as they want. The period varied, however, can only be within the timescale of the original order set by the sheriff (s 24(2)).

A sheriff can recall or vary a banning order if satisfied that there has been a change in the "facts or circumstances" from the time

---

[13] These conditions are made up of appeal timescales, the appeal being abandoned or the Court of Session agreeing with the sheriff principal to quash (reject) the order originally granted by the sheriff.

the order was granted or varied. The evidence would therefore start from the original application to show what has changed (s 24(1)). It is assumed that the court will hold the original application to allow for variation powers at a later stage. These powers under s 24 therefore reinforce the need for the original application to be as comprehensive as possible, either to challenge or to support a variation. See Chapter 7 for guidance on evidence.

Before the application to vary or recall an order is lodged the applicant has to notify, where relevant, the subject of the application and the adult (s 41(3)). If the eligible applicant to vary or recall the order happens to be the subject of the original banning order or temporary order, this may cause some distress to the adult. One would assume that the subject's solicitor would notify the adult. After the banning order or temporary banning order is varied or recalled, the notifications to all parties under s 26(2) are effected by the sheriff clerk, to prevent the adult having any contact with the original subject of the banning order.[14]

BREACHING A FULL OR TEMPORARY BANNING ORDER AND POWER OF ARREST: s 28 (BREACH) AND s 25 (POWER OF ARREST)

28 *Arrest for breach of banning order*

*(1) A constable may arrest **without warrant** the subject of any banning order, or temporary banning order, to which a **power of arrest** is attached if the constable—*

- *(a) **reasonably suspects** the subject to be **breaching**, or to have breached, the order, and*
- *(b) considers that there would, if the subject were not arrested, be **a risk of the subject breaching the order again**.*

(2) The constable must—

- *(a) immediately inform the arrested person of the reason for the arrest, and*
- *(b) **take the arrested person** as quickly as is reasonably practicable to a police station.*

Significance of wording

- **without warrant**: the power of arrest attached to the banning order is in itself sufficient authority for the police constable to take a subject into police custody;

---

[14] Amended by Act of Sederunt (Summary Applications, Statutory Applications and Appeals etc Rules) Amendment (Adult Support and Protection (Scotland) Act 2007) (No 3) (SSI 2008/375).

- **power of arrest**: s 25: this is a discretion the sheriff has to attach such a power to an order either on the initial application or at any time after the order is granted. The power of arrest authorises any constable to remove the subject to a police station, using reasonable force if necessary. The constable is not named in the power of arrest;
- **reasonably suspects**: the evidence for the constable to use the power of arrest would be if the adult, or preferably someone else, has witnessed the subject of the order breaching the conditions in the order. Even one eyewitness and an admission from the subject, where possible, would be sufficient evidence to use the power of arrest. The subject may no longer be at the adult's house. If found elsewhere this is also sufficient credible evidence that the order has been breached. Any evidence must be corroborated, ie there must be more than one source of evidence;
- **breaching**: this is non-compliance with the order itself in s 19(1) or any of the conditions attached to the order in s 19(2);[15]
- **a risk of the subject breaching the order again**: if the subject has been at the adult's specified place, for example, day centre or their home, several times before the police had been informed; or the subject's attitude suggests that they will ignore a warning to stay away; or the subject is threatening the adult, then this would be sufficient evidence to use the power of arrest. It is likely that the constable would err on the side of caution by using the power of arrest to protect the adult;
- **take the arrested person**: the arrested subject would be taken to a police station then kept in custody, to appear in court on the next lawful court day. This could be anything from a few hours to a few days later, depending on the time of the arrest.

Where a banning order has a power of arrest attached, the police officer – legally termed the "constable" – can formally arrest the subject of an order without using a warrant if any of the conditions in s 19(1) or (2) quoted above is breached. Before doing so, the applicant needs to request that a power of arrest be attached to the order. The sheriff then has the discretion to attach a power of arrest at the same time as granting a banning order or a temporary banning order or at a later stage upon application (s 25(1)).

---

[15] See Code of Practice, Chapter 11, paras 59–63 for further details.

It is not clear from the Act, however, whether this right later to apply for a power of arrest belongs only to the original applicant. If not, then another party may have to use the right to vary the order using s 24(1), and have a power of arrest attached where good cause is shown. The parties who can apply to vary or recall a banning order or a temporary banning order are listed in s 24(3).[16]

Where a power of arrest is attached to an order of any kind – full, temporary, varied or recalled – the applicant has to inform the chief constable under s 27. This notification triggers stored police information when the power of arrest is used. The constable can exercise discretion in s 28(1) above before using the power of arrest where the subject has already breached the order; is in the process of breaching the order; or is likely to breach the order again if not arrested.

The Act is silent on the timescales between the breach itself and using the power of arrest. Standard operational procedures in each force should state police guidance on what action to take to search for the subject after a breach of the order – whether this is after a few hours or a few days.

The Act is equally silent on what action should be taken by the constable should the subject not be arrested but has still breached the order. The subject may have breached the order several times over a few days or weeks and no action may have been taken by individual constables. Standard operational procedures for separate breaches without follow-up powers of arrest may advise that all breaches are recorded at a central database within a force. The subject could then be informed of this procedure at the time of questioning. This may itself prevent further breaches.

This accumulation of breaches would then build up evidence for a power of arrest using the s 28(1)(b) test. In short, the data on breaches of an order with or without a power of arrest should be accessible by police staff.

For further information on police action after a power of arrest is used, see Code of Practice, Chapter 11, paras 59–78.

CASE STUDY: GRACE

Grace is a 73-year-old single woman with early onset dementia. She lives alone. She has no contact with a

---

[16] This is speculation on the author's part, as a power of arrest is attached and is not part of a variation. It would therefore make sense for the original applicant to apply for a power of arrest.

brother in England who may now be deceased. Grace has been known to social services for many years because of neglecting her home. There have also been referrals from neighbours who were concerned about her gas fire being left on unlit. Grace has no sense of smell and so is unaware of this danger. The social services staff have cleaned up her house periodically but it is soon neglected again. Grace does not want a home care service. She spends long periods each day walking around the town and often appears unkempt. Following the diagnosis of early-stage dementia, the Community Psychiatric Nurse (CPN) monitors Grace.

Grace becomes friends with Ruby whom she met in a café in the town. This friendship seems to be beneficial in that Ruby starts to visit Grace regularly, although the CPN is suspicious as Grace does not usually allow visitors in her house. In time, Grace complains to the CPN about money going missing from her bank account. The CPN discovers from Grace that Ruby cashes Grace's pension. The CPN refers Grace to social services who then make a visit. Grace remembers and trusts the social worker from past visits. She shows the social worker her bank papers. Ruby's name is stated as a third-party withdrawer. Grace then remembers she agreed to this to allow Ruby to take money on her behalf in the winter when she cannot get to the bank herself. There are large withdrawals of money for this period. With Grace's permission, the social worker makes further inquiries of her bank, under Pt 2, s 47 of the Act (s 24C of the AWI Act). The bank shows evidence of withdrawals but these have been signed by Grace and countersigned by Ruby, the third party.

Is there sufficient evidence to apply for a banning order?

The council decides to "test the water" and apply for a banning order, given Grace's distress at having her money going missing. The evidence clearly points to Ruby, although perhaps not to a criminal level. Nevertheless, the bank could prove that larger sums went missing when Ruby used third-party withdrawals.

The council also lodged an application for a temporary banning order, with a condition in s 19(2)(a) that Ruby, the subject of the order, should not attempt to visit Grace at home. The council submits a "plan" specifying that Ruby should not visit Grace in her home or meet Grace in the town (SI 1999/929, r 3.35.3). The council also requests a power of arrest under s 25 should Ruby breach this condition.

The council witnesses were the CPN, the CO (social worker) and the Old Age Psychiatrist who initially diagnosed Grace's dementia. The psychiatrist also confirmed Grace's incapacity to consent to the banning order. The sheriff clerk served notice on Ruby, who chose not to attend the court or to be legally represented using her right under s 41(4) of the Act.

Court actions

The sheriff granted a temporary banning order to prevent Ruby from visiting Grace. The sheriff used his discretion under s 25(1) not to attach a power of arrest, on the ground that Ruby was not represented as a party in court. The sheriff did, however, use his own discretion under s 19(2)(f) to ban Ruby from going near Grace's bank. He added a further condition by banning Ruby from taking money from Grace's account by third-party means. The council indicated that it would use the powers in Pt 2 of the Act to apply to the OPG to intromit with Grace's account. This would take up to 1 month to effect.

Given the medical proof of Grace's incapacity, the sheriff appointed a safeguarder using his powers under s 41(6), with a remit to investigate the circumstances between Grace and Ruby (s 41(7)). Using his power under s 21(3), the sheriff set a hearing date 6 weeks later, to consider the banning order.

At the full hearing to consider a banning order, the parties were the (safeguarder acting on behalf of the court) and the council, with the same witnesses as before. Ruby was not present but chose to have a solicitor represent her in terms of s 41(4).

The sheriff heard from Ruby's solicitor that she had not breached the temporary banning order during this 6-week period. This was confirmed by the council who stated that it had checked with the police for any record of a breach. The safeguarder stated that he had interviewed Grace, Ruby and the council's witnesses. He confirmed that Grace was an "adult at risk".

Court decision: two possible outcomes

1. The sheriff recalled the temporary banning order under s 21(4)(b) and chose not to grant a full banning order because of the safeguarder's evidence and the fact that Ruby had not breached the temporary banning order. The council also assured the sheriff that it had financial control of Grace's bank account, using the "intromission with funds" power in Pt 2, s 58 (s 25 of the AWI Act). A certificate from the OPG was shown as evidence.

2. The sheriff imposed a 4-month banning order with the same conditions as in the temporary banning order. However, the sheriff advised the parties of their right to apply for the banning order to be recalled under s 24 which this time included Ruby, the subject of the order. The sheriff added that a safeguarder would then be appointed with any application.

Further legal action: Pt 2 of the Act

Given Grace's incapacity, the social services department became her DWP appointee. A care package was set up, involving home care services to help Grace with her money. As described above, the council had control of Grace's bank account using Pt 2 of the Act.

6 URGENT USE OF PROTECTION ORDERS

The Act provides for applications using the justice of the peace court system where an adult has to be removed or visited on an urgent basis. This default application is used where it is not practical to access a sheriff or where any delay will harm an adult further.

The Scottish Court Service now administers the justice of the peace system. Access should be through the local sheriff court and not the local authority. The separate Bench and signing justice of the peace (JP) roles have been amalgamated into one role. It may be that JP courts will be sitting within the sheriff courts but this may vary across Scotland.[1]

The Act gives the JP following emergency powers:

(1) to grant a removal order for 24 hours;
(2) automatically to attach a 12-hour warrant to enter in order to use the removal order;
(3) to grant a warrant to enter a place being visited under s 7.

These circumstances could feasibly arise after office hours. Non-statutory forms for this purpose are available from the Scottish Government adult protection website. Given that they are non-statutory, they can be adapted to suit any circumstances.

The applicant to the JP for exercise of any of the powers can be any council employee and not necessarily a CO as in normal court applications. For example, this could be a council solicitor. The person implementing either an urgent removal order or a warrant must still be a CO as per normal procedures. A council nominee, however, can also conduct the actual moving of the adult (s 14(1)(a)).

The key components in a JP application are discussed using the following headings:

• Urgent applications – definition
• Summary points for (i) removal order; (ii) warrant to enter
• Application forms.

---

[1] Justices of the Peace (Scotland) Order 2007 (SSI 2007/210). See, eg, Justice of the Peace Courts (Sheriffdom of South Strathclyde, Dumfries and Gallloway) Order 2009 (SSI 2009/115), for commencement dates for some Scottish courts.

URGENT APPLICATIONS – DEFINITION: s 40

40 Urgent cases

(1) A council which believes that the circumstances set out in subsection (2) have arisen may apply to a justice of the peace instead of the sheriff for—

> *(a) a removal order, **or***
> *(b) a warrant for entry in respect of a visit under **section 7.***

(2) Those circumstances are—

> *(a) that it is **not practicable** to apply to the sheriff, and*
> *(b) that an adult at risk is likely to be harmed if there is any **delay** in granting such an order or warrant.*

...

(8) Despite section 37(2)(a), a warrant for entry granted under this section expires 12 hours after it is granted.

Significance of wording

- **section 7**: This is the CO's statutory right to visit an adult, allowing the CO to visit if he knows or believes that any adult is an "adult at risk" using the s 3 criteria and may need protection from harm;
- **not practicable**: the interpretation for this term will depend on each case. The argument to the JP could be, for example, either that the court was closed or that a sheriff was not available to hear the evidence. This argument is coupled with preventing the likelihood of further harm to the "adult at risk";
- **delay**: this is linked to urgency and the argument for an expedient solution to prevent the likelihood of harm as defined in s 53(1).

SUMMARY POINTS FOR (i) REMOVAL ORDER; (ii) WARRANT TO ENTER

Removal order: s 40(1)(a)

The council can apply to a JP for a removal order. The JP is also obliged automatically to grant a warrant for entry to help gain access to the adult's place where access is denied (s 40(5)). The criteria for using the warrant are already justified in the removal order application itself, hence the reason for the warrant being automatic. The immediate criterion for applying to a JP as opposed to the sheriff is urgency. This means that the council has to prove to the justice: (1) that it is not practical to apply for a removal order using the court system; and (2) that the adult at risk is likely to be harmed if there is a delay in a court application. Examples of this could be location, court schedules and the time of day when a removal order is needed (s 40(2)). However, the criterion to justify a removal order is the same as for a court application where s 40(3)(b) cross-refers to s 15(1).

The periods for implementing, exercising and sustaining a removal order are shorter than for court orders – 12 hours to implement and only 24 hours to sustain a removal order. This compares with 72 hours and up to 7 days using a court removal order.

Similarly, the time for implementing a warrant for entry for an urgent application is reduced to 12 hours compared with 72 hours for a court warrant. The reason for these shorter periods is that the rights to be notified in advance by the council and later heard by the sheriff are removed when granted by a justice. They would therefore be used only in urgent circumstances to prevent the likelihood of harm (s 40(2)(b)).

The council may then wish to re-apply for a removal order using the court system if a longer period is required. The specified place to which the council chooses to remove the person on an urgent basis using s 40 may therefore be different for a court application under s 15(1). Given that the adult has already been moved on an urgent basis, the council may request that the court disapply the standard notifications under s 40(2) in order to keep the adult from the original place of harm.

Warrant for entry for a s 7 visit: s 40(1)(b)

The prerequisite for an assessment order is a statutory visit under s 7. If access were refused then a s 37 warrant for entry would be applied for at the local court.

In urgent circumstances, however, the council can apply to a JP for a warrant to enter to undertake a s 7 visit. A JP cannot grant an assessment order but this visit may lead to using either an assessment order or a removal order, depending on the outcome.

The wording in a s 40(1)(b) warrant for a s 7 visit is the same as for a s 37 warrant but the warrant is signed by a justice instead of a sheriff.

The immediate criterion for applying to a JP as opposed to the sheriff is urgency. This means that the council has to prove to the JP: (1) that it is not practical to apply for a warrant using the court system; and (2) that the adult at risk is likely to be harmed if there is a delay in a court application.

Examples of this could be location, court schedules and the time of day when an order or a warrant is needed.

The council also has to show evidence that access to the adult's place is likely to be refused or there are other reasons why the council is unable to enter or that a warrant is necessary because of failed previous attempts to gain access (s 38(2)).

The time for implementation of a warrant for entry for an urgent application is reduced to 12 hours, compared with 72 hours for a court application.

APPLICATION FORMS

These are available from the Adult Protection Act website created by the Scottish Government: http://www.scotland.gov.uk/Topics/Health/care/VAUnit/jpguidance

There is also a useful website from the same source which discusses entry and removal powers, followed by the JP peace forms: http://www.scotland.gov.uk/Resource/Doc/924/0067143.doc

As for all warrants, these come in pairs – the application and the actual warrant signed by the JP.

JP01 – application for a warrant for entry in relation to a visit;

JP02 – warrant for entry in relation to a visit;

JP03 – application for a removal order;

JP03 – removal order – warrant for entry to be issued at the same time.

Unlike court protection orders, the forms listed above are non-statutory which means that they can be altered to suit the relevant circumstances.

QUESTIONS FROM PROFESSIONALS[2]

1. If a justice of the peace removal order is issued (lasting only 24 hours), is it competent then (after 24 hours) to apply to a sheriff for a removal order (which, if approved, could last up to 7 days)? This arises as, if the person is at such urgent risk (to justify application to JP) then the fact that a JP order last only 24 hours seems a "contradiction". This effectively becomes an "interim removal order", ie for the first 24 hours with a view to then applying for a sheriff's order that could last for 7 days.

---

[2] This is from a selection of questions raised by professionals' training sessions for the Act. They came from Ian Kinsley, Care Training Matters Ltd. The original phraseology is intact. The responses are from this author.

2. If the presenting risk is so high and you cannot wait for a sheriff, why make the order so short? This strikes me as a mistake unless it is an interim position. If it was intended as an interim position then why should the Act not be more explicit about a provision to apply for a full application to the sheriff? If that is the case, perhaps the urgent application should be longer, ie 72 hours instead of 24 hours.

RESPONSE

The Act does not prohibit the use of repeat applications for a removal order. If the criteria still apply then it would be for the sheriff to decide on its appropriateness. I think it would sound like a joined-up "recipe" if the Act were too prescriptive.

The sheriff can limit the period of the removal order for any application for up to 7 days. The council therefore still needs to produce evidence of benefit and of least restriction in order to justify any period. This evidence is challengeable using the notification to parties court procedure in s 41. The Act has restricted an urgent removal order to 24 hours because it cannot be so challenged.

7 PROTECTION ORDERS – GUIDANCE ON COURT PROCEDURES

The following is a discussion of the kinds of evidence that will best support a council in applying for a protection order. It would be good practice, before considering a protection order, to hold a case conference to consider other options, in keeping with the "least restrictive" principle. The application will probably be drafted by a council solicitor, based on information from professionals involved in the adult's life. The evidence below is therefore an attempt to encapsulate this range of information.

For ease of reading, the evidence will be subdivided into the following headings. These points are summaries of information already in the previous chapters on protection orders. They may also be repeated within each section.

- Consent of adult at risk.
- General and guiding principles – application.
- Shared evidence for all applications.
- Additional evidence for each order and warrants.

CONSENT OF ADULT AT RISK: s 35

A statement should be included as to whether the subject of the application has consented to it, if the adult has capacity. If not, the sheriff then has to decide whether there is evidence of "undue pressure" in terms of s 35(3). Undue pressure could come from someone the adult is afraid of or being threatened by. It could also come from a person not suspected of harming the adult, for example someone placing undue pressure on him not to consent – even perhaps trying to cover up for someone else. In short, the council is evidencing "undue pressure" and not capacity.

If the adult cannot consent because of mental incapacity then medical evidence should be produced to prove this, as in applications for guardianship orders using the AWI Act. This guidance is repeated throughout the Code of Practice for each protection order, as follows: "Where the adult does not have capacity to consent, the requirement to prove undue pressure does not apply. However evidence of lack of incapacity will be required by the Sheriff."[1]

If the adult already has a proxy under the AWI Act with relevant powers related to court applications, they can substitute for the adult's consent, provided that they are not the suspected harmer. The inclusion of this Act in a power of attorney or welfare, financial or property guardianship orders could be a standard power. Suggested wording:

> "To consent to any order on the adult's behalf in terms of the Adult Support and Protection (Scotland) Act 2007 where the guardian/ attorney considers it appropriate."

Where the adult has incapacity, and no proxy under the AWI Act, the council may wish to consider applying for a welfare guardianship using its default duty under s 57(2) of the AWI Act.

GENERAL AND GUIDING PRINCIPLES – APPLICATION

The two guiding principles of benefit and of least restriction in s 1 must be evidenced, probably in terms of the degree of harm the adult would suffer if not subject to the protection order. Evidence from a medical or a financial source may be appropriate, depending on the type of harm from which the adult is to be protected. Evidence supporting the general principles, including past and present wishes of the adult, should be produced where possible. The same approach could be adopted in relation to the adult's nearest relative, primary carer, guardian, attorney or any other person having an interest in the adult's well-being or property (listed in s 2(c)). If possible, it would be helpful to have the statement of the adult's wishes signed and witnessed by the CO undertaking the initial inquiry under s 4.

SHARED EVIDENCE FOR ALL APPLICATIONS

The following paragraphs relate to information that will be familiar to social work staff in the course of doing risk assessments as they use their local procedures. The information could be presented in summary form to support the evidence for care and protection.

State the source of the referral and why the order is being sought. It may also be useful to state which alternatives were considered, ruled out and why.

---

[1] Code of Practice, Chapter 9, para 25; Chapter 10, para 14; Chapter 11, para 42.

The adult's current state of mental or physical health; current accommodation/finances; family history (where relevant); social contacts, for example family or friends; a formal care plan from any statutory or voluntary organisations; the adult's ability to self-care; substance abuse/offending history, where relevant; and financial, ethnic, cultural and religious factors relevant to the application.

The evidence for the adult to be an "adult at risk" depends on two legal tests: (1) knowledge; and (2) belief (s 4). The applicant should therefore distinguish their evidence for each test, which would depend on the nature of the harm, for example from health or financial sources such as the adult's doctor or banker. This written or oral evidence could be used to support any of the three-pronged definitions of "adult at risk" in s 3(1), thereby focusing the argument on what aspect of risk the sheriff has to address.

Similarly, the evidence for harm should focus on the definition of harm in s 53(1) of the Act, ie conduct which causes physical or psychological harm; harm to property such as theft, fraud, embezzlement or extortion; or self-harm. In the latter case, there should be evidence of whose actions, or non-actions, have led the adult to self-harm.

The evidence to support the legal test of "serious harm" is included in each application for a protection order and relates to the legal term "risk" (s 12(a); s 15(1)(a)); s 20(a)). This could be in summary form from the comprehensive risk assessments used in local authority procedures.[2]

A summary of multi-agency assessments and recommendations of case conferences could also be included.

Discuss the reasons for and outcomes of previous protection order applications and orders under other parallel legislation such as the AWI Act or the 2003 Act, where relevant. State what efforts and services made to support the adult previously and how it helped or not in terms of reducing harm. Discuss what council duty of support is being given to the adult and what appropriate services have been considered (s 6(2)).

Provide proof of standard court procedures in terms of notifications of the application to the subject of the application and the adult. Names and addresses/telephone contacts should be supplied in the summary application to enable the court in turn to fulfil its legal obligations to invite parties to attend under s 41(4) (s 41(3)).

---

[2] The ultimate power to interpret "serious" lies with the sheriff. The applicant should therefore not presuppose either way the strength of their evidence.

The council can choose to request that the sheriff disapply any or all of the standard court procedures listed in s 41(3)–(7). The evidence must apply specifically to each procedure the sheriff is being asked to waive and be shown to protect the adult from serious harm or not to prejudice any person affected by the disapplication. This could be, for example, where the adult's immediate safety is at risk and the court needs to grant any of the three orders more speedily (s 41(2)).

The sheriff can dispense with an adult's consent to any protection order application if the council can prove that the adult is subject to "undue pressure" from a person suspected of inflicting harm toward that adult. The level of proof required is that the sheriff must "reasonably believe" that undue pressure from any person has stopped the adult from giving consent and that no other reasonable steps to protect the adult from further harm have worked (s 35(3)). To do this, the council has to prove that the adult's confidence and trust in the suspected harmer is affecting his ability to give consent to the order. This undue pressure relationship could also apply to any other person in whom the adult has trust and confidence, such as a relative, a neighbour or a carer (s 35(5)).[3] The source of evidence could be the adult directly or could arise in the process of interviewing any other adult found in the place during the investigation. This process could be quite wide ranging and include relatives, friends, care providers or relevant professional staff. The CO may therefore wish to take statements from these persons by way of providing evidence of undue pressure (s 8(1)).

If the adult has been medically proved not to have capacity to consent to the application for the order then the "undue pressure" test does not apply. This medical evidence for incapacity will instead be used in support of a protection order. The Act therefore gives support and protection for adults regardless of capacity.

The council too has to consider whether the adult or any other key witness is a vulnerable witness in terms of the VW Act. The key issue is whether the quality of the evidence is marred in terms of completeness, coherence and accuracy if the witness is over-anxious and feeling under pressure in court. The decision on whether or not to provide special measures in court to improve the giving of evidence rests entirely with the sheriff. This too can be considered at any stage in the court proceedings.[4]

---

[3] Code of Practice, Chapter 9, para 24.
[4] See Appendix 3 for details on the Vulnerable Witnesses (Scotland) Act 2004.

ADDITIONAL EVIDENCE FOR EACH PROTECTION ORDER AND WARRANTS

The above is an outline of shared evidence for each protection order. The following is suggested evidence specific to each type of protection order. This will help the applicant to direct evidence to the available options in the separate orders.

Assessment order: s 11

It is worth stating in the application why the assessment cannot be completed in the adult's home. The phrase used in s 13 is "due to lack of privacy or otherwise", thus leaving the council with a wide scope for interpretation.

The application should comment on why the place being used for the assessment order is suitable. For example, if this is in a local authority resource or a contracted resource, then the service provider could prepare a statement on its suitability. In terms of the medical examination, more than one place may be used (such as a health clinic or perhaps later a hospital to carry out more tests). This may require separate statements.[5]

The right to move an adult for an assessment order lies solely with the CO (s 11(1)). Section 38(1) states that the sheriff must routinely grant a warrant for entry with an assessment order. No evidence is required for this warrant. Police presence can therefore be a useful option. If the CO chooses to be accompanied by any other person to carry out the assessment order, then only the adult, and not the court, can allow him to enter the adult's place.

Where appropriate, the application should also state the council nominee who is to interview the adult, for example a key worker, community nurse or other person already known to the adult (s 11(1)(a)).

Section 11(1) affords the council a choice of interviewers for the assessment order. It may be that a joint interview between the CO and the council nominee is necessary. The reasons for this should therefore be stated in the application, to allow the adult or any other relevant party to challenge them using standard court procedure in s 41(4).

Removal order: s 14

For further guidance on proving s 3(1) and availability and suitability of a place, see the first paragraph under assessment order guidance above (s 15(1) and (2)).

---

[5] The Code of Practice is silent on this possibility.

Section 16(1) allows a CO to remove an adult from "any place" to a specified place cited in the removal order. The adult may have a tenancy or be living in non-specific circumstances such as a hostel or with the subject. At worst, the adult may run away or be abducted by another person.

The right to move an adult for a removal order can be done by either a CO or another person nominated by the council. The right to enter any place in order to remove an adult using s 16, however, applies only to the CO. The adult would therefore have to permit the council nominee to enter his place to help effect the move.

If a council nominee is being used to help remove the adult, the application should state their names and why they are being nominated (s 14(1)(a)).

If the council is applying for conditions within the removal order, these should be stated: who, when, why and in what circumstances (for example, under supervision arrangements, including named places and detailed times) (s 15(2)).

Although not legally required, the council should consider having an access and support plan included in the application as contingency arrangements during and beyond the removal order.[6]

The sheriff or justice of the peace must routinely grant a warrant for entry to a removal order. No evidence is required for this warrant. Police presence can therefore be a useful option (ss 39(1) and 40(5)).

Banning order: s 19

The evidence for "well-being or property" would have to be evidenced in relation to what is the least restrictive and beneficial legal action for the adult at risk, ie why the adult should not be moved instead. The phrase "better safeguarded" is the key to this argument (s 20(b)).[7]

The applicant should have copies of the adult's tenancy or sub-tenancy agreement, to prove occupancy rights. If the subject and adult are living together and the subject has sole occupancy rights, then the subject cannot be banned. If neither the adult nor the subject has occupancy rights in a place, then the subject can be banned (s 20(c)). Section 23 provides for the interpretation of occupancy rights by way of the Matrimonial Homes (Family Protection) (Scotland) Act 1981 ("MH Act") to ensure that the adult cannot ban someone who is entitled to occupancy where the adult is not so entitled.

---

[6] Code of Practice, Chapter 10, para 42.
[7] *Ibid*, Chapter 11, para 20.

The MH Act was amended by the Civil Partnership Act 2004 to ensure that the MH Act applies to civil partners in exactly the same way as it applies to married couples. The MH Act also applies to cohabiting heterosexual couples. In short, the banning order applies to both domestic and non-domestic settings where there is no requirement for the adult or subject to be related or even be a partner.

These legal permutations are complex, to say the least. The council legal services department should advise on the type of proof required to evidence eligibility of both the adult and the subject of the order.

There is a legal requirement in the regulations for the applicant to include a "plan" that clearly identifies the area from which the subject is being banned or the place from which subject is being ejected. These areas or places could be public or private (s 19(2)(a) ("specified area") or s 19(2)(b) ("summary ejection")).[8]

The applicant could include the following information as a guide for the conditions within the banning or temporary banning order.

1. The length of time the applicant wishes the banning order to last and the reasons for this (s 19(5)).

2. Where a temporary banning order is co-lodged, the reasons for this and the length of time requested.

3. Conditions of contact, ie who, when, why and in what circumstances, for example under supervision (s 19(3)).

4. Actions being taken where the subject of the banning order is a child (s 30(2)).

5. Where appropriate, reasons for a blanket banning order with no conditions, for example persistent harm or a court case pending. This is the opposite of supervised contact where harm can be reduced by conciliation.

6. What action will be taken to support a banned person where they too may require support?

7. Where a previous order has been applied for, details of this and whether it was granted and the outcome.

8. Proposed actions under any other legislation, for example guardianship application or intromission of funds (s 4(b) uses the term "or otherwise").[9]

---

[8] Act of Sederunt (Summary Applications, Statutory Applications and Appeals etc) Rules 1999 (SI 1999/929), r 3.35.3, inserted by SI 2008/335, para 2.

[9] Part 2 of this Act amends the Adults with Incapacity (Scotland) Act 2000 to have more financial powers such as intromission of funds. See Chapter 8 for specific procedures to exercise these powers.

9. What support is being given to the adult during the period of the order? This could be established by a s 7(1) visit, ie "to decide whether it needs to do anything (by performing functions under this Part or otherwise)".

10. Reasons for any request to the sheriff to disapply notifications (s 41(2)).

11. Where relevant, what actions have been taken to preserve any moveable property owned or controlled by the subject that remains in the specified place while the order has effect? Has the subject agreed to this in writing (s 19(2)(d))?

12. Consideration of co-lodging an application for special measures under the Vulnerable Witnesses (Scotland) Act 2004.

Warrant for entry: s 37

Given that a warrant is granted automatically if either an assessment order or a removal order is granted, the bulk of the information will already be available (s 38(1) for an assessment order; s 39(1) for a removal order).

However, the council has to provide separate evidence if it wishes to carry out a s 7 visit alone. The sole legal test therefore is for the council to prove that it "reasonably suspects" that entry will be refused or that some other circumstance may arise to frustrate entry. The evidence for this is open ended and subject to variation (s 38(2)).[10]

It should be noted that the terms of the warrant in s 37(1)(b) give a constable wider powers than just opening lockfast premises. Instead, the Act uses the phrase "to do anything, using reasonable force where necessary" to describe the police powers. In other words, the powers have no limitations in application (s 37(1)(b)).[11]

The warrants are included as Schedule 1 to SI 1999/929 as Form 35 (as inserted by SSI 2008/335, para 2).

---

[10] Code of Practice, Chapter 5, para 20.

[11] *Ibid*, Chapter 5, para 26 discusses the local authority duty to secure the safety of the adult's premises and belongings if force has been used to gain access. This should be a joint police/local authority duty prescribed by local procedures.

8 2007 ACT, PART 2 (ADULTS WITH INCAPACITY)

Part 2 of the 2007 Act amends the AWI Act to improve how it operates in practice. This arose from a 2-year project monitoring the implementation of the AWI Act, resulting in a consultation paper, "Improving with Experience", issued by the Scottish Executive in August 2005.

These changes were made because of their relevance to the subject of adult protection, this time focusing on adults with incapacity who may be "adults at risk". They include allowing a council to intromit with the funds of an adult with incapacity. These new powers therefore allow a council to widen its scope in supporting and protecting adults with incapacity. Other amendments are powers of attorney, intervention orders and guardianship orders. Although these relate more to adults with incapacity, they will be discussed briefly here.

The chapter is in two parts: (1) a brief outline of the major amendments in the AWI Act; (2) how a council can use Pt 2 of this Act to intromit with the funds of an adult with incapacity. This will be useful information where an adult at risk is being harmed financially.

OUTLINE OF KEY CHANGES TO THE AWI ACT AS AMENDED BY PT 2 OF ACT

The main amendments discussed are as follows:[1]

(a) powers of attorney;
(a) intromission with funds; using Pt 3 of the AWI Act;
(c) guardianship and intervention orders;
(d) other changes.

Powers of attorney: Pt 2 of AWI, ss 15–24

The changes are:[2]

---

[1] This list is by no means exhaustive. See the OPG website for fuller details: http://www.publicguardian-scotland.gov.uk/.
[2] Legal references in brackets are to Pt 2 of the Act.

- All powers of attorney that continue or begin when the adult has incapacity must now contain a statement that the granter – the adult – has "considered" how incapacity is to be, determined, to allow the attorney – the person who acts on behalf of the adult – to perform the powers in the power of attorney. The granter does not have to specify what, if any, medical assessments are to be completed in order to confirm his incapacity. If no instructions are included in the power of attorney document, then there is still scope for misuse by an attorney. The council may wish to inquire about the details of a power of attorney where financial harm is suspected (Pt 2, s 57(1)(a) and (2)(a)).

- The OPG now sends notification of welfare powers of attorney to local authorities and to the MWC. These include changes to a welfare power of attorney. A CO using his s 10 examination of records power can contact the OPG direct for a copy of the powers.

Access to funds: Pt 3 of AWI Act (Intromission with funds: ss 25–34)

The changes are:

- The arrangements for countersigning of applications are more flexible. The countersignatory will no longer have to be a member of a prescribed class and will not need to know the adult. However, they will need to have known the applicant for at least 1 year (rather than 2 years, as before) and state that the applicant is a "fit and proper person" to intromit with funds.

- More flexible arrangements for managing the bank accounts of adults with incapacity and transferring funds between accounts.

- Provision for the OPG to authorise banks to release information about an adult's account and also to open an account to enable an application to be taken forward (see below for practice guidelines).

- Provision for joint and reserve withdrawers to overcome current difficulties when a withdrawer is unable to act.

- Organisations, as well as individuals, will be able to use the scheme.

- More streamlined arrangements for renewing authority to access to funds and moving from financial guardianship to access to funds.

Guardianship and intervention orders

The changes are:

- To allow sheriffs to dispense with caution where appropriate (caution is a type of insurance to safeguard the adult's estate from any loss caused by the actions of the intervener or guardian, but it can be disproportionately expensive and difficult to obtain); and to permit other forms of security to be accepted by the Public Guardian instead of caution.

- Discretion for sheriffs to accept medical reports issued more than 30 days previously, in certain circumstances.

- A regulatory provision to enable Ministers to prescribe new classes of medical practitioners who can sign the second medical certificate for applications where incapacity is caused by mental disorder.

- Where an adult lives outwith Scotland and lacks capacity because of a mental disorder, a suitably qualified local practitioner to be able to visit and to prepare the second report after discussion with an officer or Commissioner of the Mental Welfare Commission for Scotland.

- Sheriffs to be able to make interim orders for a period of more than 3 months and up to a maximum of 6 months, where this is appropriate in the circumstances of the case.

- A new provision allowing a guardianship order to be applied for in the 3-month period prior to a person's 16th birthday.

- A simplified renewal process for guardianships.

- Local authority to be able to recall welfare guardianships where the Chief Social Work Officer is the guardian.

- Requirement for the renewal of transitional guardianships (pre-Act curators, tutors dative and tutors-at-law), if appropriate, within 2 years.

The OPG has new powers to obtain information when carrying out investigations into the exercise of authority by proxies under the AWI Act. Proxies can be required by the OPG to provide them with their records and other relevant information. In addition, banks and other financial institutions can be required by the OPG to provide them with records and other relevant information about the accounts of the adult concerned (Act, Pt 2, s 61, inserting s 81A of the AWI Act).

There are now numbers of minor administrative changes to ensure that information is appropriately notified to the OPG.

Other changes

- Clarification of the powers of local authorities to deliver services under the Social Work (Scotland) Act 1968 to adults who lack capacity (s 64 of the Act).[3]
- A provision that in considering AWI Act applications sheriffs must take account of the views expressed on behalf of the adult by a person providing independent advocacy services (AWI Act, Pt 2, s 55).
- A provision to allow for displacement of an adult's nearest relative on an application by a person with an interest in the adult's welfare, or by the adult (AWI Act, Pt 2, s 56).
- A provision to allow the Public Guardian to take part in, or initiate, court proceedings when it appears to be necessary to safeguard an adult's property or financial affairs (AWI Act, Pt 3, s 67).
- Enhanced powers for the Public Guardian to obtain information when carrying out an investigation (AWI Act, Pt 2, s 61).

The Legal Aid (Scotland) Act 1986 is amended to allow regulations to be made so that free civil legal aid will be available for intervention or guardianship orders that relate to the personal welfare of the adult, in cases where the application is made by the adult himself (Act, Pt 5, s 77(1) and Sch 1 (part only), para 3(b)).

APPLICATION OF FINANCIAL POWERS IN PT 2 OF THE ACT

Part 3 of the AWI Act deals with accounts and funds. Families use this mainly to operate bank accounts on behalf of the adult with incapacity. The legal term is "intromission with funds". The spending is monitored by the OPG.

Part 2 of the Act updates Pt 3 of the AWI Act considerably. The amendment now allows "corporate bodies", including a local authority, to perform the same functions as for an individual. This may therefore be a useful strategy when dealing with adults at risk where financial harm is present.

The following details discuss the powers available to a local authority and how to implement them.

Practice guidance – preliminary information

1. The applicant has to complete a prescribed form from the OPG and submit a medical certificate to confirm incapacity.

---

[3] A Ward, *Adults with Incapacity Legislation* (2008) has a useful discussion on s 13ZA in Appendix I.

The OPG keeps this certificate indefinitely, thus allowing for further applications without the need to seek another certificate. The medical certificate is in the form prescribed by the Adults with Incapacity (Accounts and Funds) (Scotland) Regulations 2008 (SSI 2008/51), although it is included in the ATF forms on the OPG website. The medical practitioner is entitled to request a fee for providing the certificate.

2. If the applicant is an individual then all forms must be countersigned by an appropriate person confirming suitability to perform the powers. The key prerequisite is that the countersignatory must have known the adult for at least 12 months and deemed him a "fit and proper person" to intromit with the adult's funds.[4]

3. The OPG has discretion in checking on these people. The OPG can also refer to applications to the court where it is challenged, using s 58 (substituting s 27F of the AWI Act). Leaving that power aside, this could be a source of harm to an adult even though the OPG has monitoring and suspension powers under s 58 (substituting s 30B and s 31A of the AWI Act respectively).

4. If the applicant is an employee of a corporate body, then that body must first register its interest with the OPG which then issues a registration reference number. Employees within that public body can then use this unique number. The Director of Finance for each council would complete a "Fitness to Access Funds" form in order to register.

5. All applicants are termed "persons" after being approved to exercise financial powers. These powers are listed in Forms ATF 1–7.[5]

6. The authority to intromit with funds is valid for 3 years, with extensions without limit of time (s 58 (substituting s 31(1) of the AWI Act).

7. These financial powers are overridden by relevant intervention or guardianship orders; or a continuing power of attorney (s 58 (substituting s 31(4) of the AWI Act).

8. The OPG website advises contact with its office to assist in completing the forms, which are somewhat complex.

9. Section 58 of the Act details the powers to be substituted in the AWI Act. Both will be referred to in the following headings.

---

[4] Section 58 (s 27A of the AWI Act).
[5] All forms are available on the OPG website (http://www.publicguardian-scotland.gov.uk/) under "Forms and Publications".

Discussion of each power:

Authority to provide information about funds: s 58 (s 24C of the AWI Act)

This permits a person to take preliminary steps to inquire about an adult's bank accounts before deciding on the further actions as described below. The prescribed Form ATF 1 is issued by the OPG. Within the form there is a medical certificate to confirm the adult's incapacity. The OPG would then issue a certificate authorising a bank or building society to provide it with the necessary information.[6]

Opening an account: s 58 (s 24D of the AWI Act)

If an adult has no suitable bank account, for example only one that is in joint names with another person, the OPG may issue a certificate authorising the opening of an account in the adult's name to deal with money the adult has or income he receives, or is likely to receive, in the future. Examples include the adult's state benefits or an occupational pension.[7]

Intromission with funds: s 58 (s 26 of the AWI Act)

If the adult has numerous bank accounts then these can be streamlined into one (designated) account to withdraw from or "intromit" with. To open a designated account for this purpose, the applicant has to use Pt 2, s 58 (s 24D of the AWI Act).

Two funds can be opened: a current account to use for the adult's daily needs and the other to gain interest on more substantial savings (Pt 2, s 58 (s 26(3) of the AWI Act)). The OPG would then issue the successful applicant with a withdrawal certificate to authorise the transfer of funds from the adult's current account to the designated account.

The OPG may authorise the payment of regular bills by standing order or direct debit or the withdrawal of funds for specific purposes. The terms of the withdrawal can now be changed more easily. The applicant can access an account already solely in the adult's name or open a fresh account under s 24D (access to funds account). The Form ATF 2 is the same for both approaches. These variations are detailed in the sections following s 26.[8]

---

[6] Section 58 (s 24C of the AWI Act); OPG Form ATF 1, titled "Request Account Information".

[7] Section 58 (s 24D of the AWI Act); OPG Form ATF 2, titled "Access to Funds".

[8] Section 58 (s 26 of the AWI Act).

Office of the Public Guardian (Scotland) (OPG)

- Website: Forms and Publications: http://www.publicguardian-scotland.gov.uk/forms/intromit_with_funds.asp

- **Intromission with Funds Applications and Guidance**

  Fitness to Access Funds – Organisations only
  - ATF 1 – Request Account Information
  - ATF 2 – Access to Funds
  - AFT 3 – Additional Joint Withdrawer
  - ATF 4 – Reserve Withdrawer
  - ATF 5 – Variation of Transaction
  - ATF 6 – Renewal of Authority

- **Guidance for Withdrawers**
  - Access to Funds – A guide for Withdrawers

- Code of Practice

- **Guidance for Fundholders (banks and building societies)**
  - Access to Account Information – A Guide for Fundholders
  - Access to Funds – A Guide for Fundholders.

9 LINKS WITH AND DIFFERENCES FROM OTHER LEGISLATION

This chapter begins with a summary of the main reasons for the Act. This is followed by details of the links and differences among the Act and the other two main Scottish statutes: the AWI Act and the 2003 Act. The contrasts are discussed using the headings:

- Main reasons for the Act
- Principles
- Investigations, inquiries and co-operation
- Actions following the investigations
- Who carries out the actions?
- If access is refused – warrants.

MAIN REASONS FOR THE ACT

The AWI Act does not have emergency powers to intervene when someone is at risk. Without this Act, no urgent intervention can take place. This Act fills the gap where there is uncertainty over the authority to intervene where apparent lack of capacity had not been or could not be determined. These are cases where the Mental Welfare Commission investigated and recommended that this legislation was required (for example Miss P; Mr H; Mr B).[1]

Both this Act and the 2003 Act can be used where an adult has a mental disorder. The 2003 Act gives the adult compulsory treatment while being detained in hospital. If the adult's vulnerability is not caused by his mental disorder, this Act should be used rather than the 2003 Act. The adult too then has a say in whether he wishes to be supported and protected using this Act.[2]

Given the investigative powers in this Act to visit using s 7, it may be more appropriate to use this power to provide both the time and protection to determine whether the grounds

---

[1] See Mental Welfare Commission website under "Investigations reports".
[2] The term "vulnerability" is used here in reference to the definition of "adult at risk" in the Act, ie "are more vulnerable to being harmed than adults who are not so affected" (s 3(1)(c)).

for compulsion under the 2003 Act are met. The visit could be followed by a medical examination for this purpose.

PRINCIPLES

Links

The shared principles in all three Acts are: benefit; least restriction; considering the wishes and feelings of the adult; and views of the adult's carer, nearest relative, attorney and guardian.

Links between this Act and the 2003 Act are: adult participation; provision of information and support; non-discrimination; and equal opportunities.

Differences

The 2003 Act has the following additional principles linked to its specific client group: to consider a range of alternative options; provision of appropriate services; and considering views of the adult's named person defined in s 250 of the 2003 Act.

INVESTIGATIONS, INQUIRIES AND CO-OPERATION FROM OTHER PUBLIC BODIES

- Each Act has a local authority duty to investigate in specific ways. The AWI Act focuses on adults who lack the mental capacity to look after their welfare, finance or property. The 2003 Act allows compulsory care and treatment for any person with a mental disorder. This Act considers adults at risk of harm from other people, including adults with incapacity and adults who have a mental disorder.
- Each Act grants powers of formal investigation where an adult's welfare or property seems to be at risk.
- Each Act gives the investigator powers to progress their inquiry through co-operation from other agencies such as the Mental Welfare Commission, the Public Guardian's Office, the Care Commission and police forces.[3]
- This Act provides further statutory powers to allow a designated council officer (CO) to make a formal visit to any place where he knows or believes that harm is being done to an adult at risk.
- The purpose of the visit is to establish whether any action needs to be taken to protect that adult from harm. As an extension to this visiting power, the CO can then proceed

---

[3] The range of statutory co-operation varies within each Act. See separate references as follows: (1) AWI Act, s 12; (2) 2003 Act, s 30; 2007 Act, s 5.

to interview any person found in a place being visited under s 7. The CO can also arrange a medical examination of any adult suspected of being an adult at risk. Information from these three investigations can be used to apply the other two statutes, for example a guardianship order or compulsory detention. See below for a summary of functions.

- The caveat to using the interviewing and medical examination powers is that an adult or any linked person can refuse to answer all or any questions in the interview. The adult can also refuse to be medically examined.

ACTIONS FOLLOWING THE INVESTIGATIONS

Each Act provides legislation to act on its investigations, as follows:

- *The Act*: there are three protection orders, as follows: (1) assessment order to take the adult from their place for up to 7 days to assess them for either an interview or a medical examination; (2) a removal order to take the adult from any source of harm for up to 7 days; (3) a banning order to prevent a person who has harmed an adult from being near the adult for up to 6 months. There can be up to six conditions attached to this order;
- *AWI Act*: intromission with funds, intervention or guardianship orders to protect the adult's welfare/finance or property. The local authority has a default duty to use financial powers;[4]
- *2003 Act*: civil detention powers for any person with a mental disorder either in hospital or in the community for care and treatment for varying periods.[5] This Act allows the removal of an adult with a diagnosed mental disorder to a place of safety lasting for up to 7 days or shorter.

WHO CARRIES OUT THE ACTIONS?

- *The Act*: a council can apply for an assessment or a removal order. With banning orders the adult suspected of harm or any person who is entitled to occupy the place concerned can apply. The council has only a default duty to apply if no-one else is likely to apply (s 22(1)(c));

---

[4] See Chapter 8 for discussion of these powers.
[5] These periods range from 72 hours, 28 days, 6 months and 12 months; also for an indefinite period for patients who are subject to a restriction order as a mentally disordered offender.

- *AWI Act*: any member of the public claiming an interest in an adult's property, financial or welfare can use this Act, as described above. The local authority too has a default duty to make applications if no other persons are willing or able to do so;
- *2003 Act*: only a mental health officer can apply for civil compulsory powers or give consent to the two shorter detention certificates.

IF ACCESS IS REFUSED – WARRANTS

The purpose and timescales for each warrant are similar:

- *The Act*: there is one warrant for two purposes in s 37:
    - a warrant to enter premises to do a s 7 visit which may then lead to an interview and a medical examination;
    - a warrant to implement an assessment order or a removal order;
- *AWI Act*: this is not applicable as there are no emergency procedures;
- *2003 Act*: there are 8-day warrants to enter premises and interview or medically examine an adult suspected of having a mental disorder. Where this is confirmed, a 7-day removal order can be used to remove that adult to a place of safety. A different warrant is used where a person is already subject to compulsory powers. The timescales in these circumstances are not prescribed.

Appendix 1
GLOSSARY

The interpretation guidance in this glossary is intended to provide readers with a ready reference only. Some of the following terms are included in the statutory definitions in s 53 of the Act. These are referenced in brackets.

Act

> The Adult Support and Protection (Scotland) Act 2007. Fully implemented in October 2008.

Adjacent place

> This may mean where the adult is living within a building. This could also mean garages/outbuildings etc (s 7(2): visits; s 16(2): removal order; s 37(1)(a): warrant to enter).

Adult

> A person aged 16 or over (s 53). The term "adult" is used to describe an "adult at risk" and an "affected adult at risk" in this book. (See also "Person" below.)

Adult at risk

> This is a legal definition in s 3, as follows:
>
> An adult who:
> - is unable to safeguard his own well-being, property, rights or other interests;
> - is at risk of harm, **and**
> - is affected by disability, mental disorder, illness or physical or mental infirmity, and consequently is more vulnerable to being harmed than adults who are not so affected (ss 3 and 53).

Adult Protection Committee (APC)

> This is a committee established by a council to safeguard adults at risk in its area. It has a responsibility to review the procedures and practices of relevant public bodies and office-holders; to give them information or advice, or make proposals;

to make or be involved in making arrangements for improving the skills and knowledge of relevant officers or employees; and any other related function specified by Ministers (ss 42 and 53).

Affected adult at risk

The word "affected" is used in s 3(1)(c) to describe the type of conditions that deem such adults "adults at risk", ie people with disability, mental disorder, illness or physical or mental infirmity. This makes them more vulnerable to harm than adults who are not so affected.

The presence of a particular condition does not automatically mean that an adult is an "adult at risk". Someone could have a disability but be able to safeguard their well-being etc. It is important to stress that all three limbs of the definition in s 3 are met, as described under "Adult at risk".

Any place

A removal order application may have the adult's current address recorded but the same order allows the council to remove the adult at risk from any place. This could mean any place within the sherrifdom where the court application is lodged. The emphasis is therefore on the word "any" (s 16: removal order).

Assessment order

A protection order granted by a sheriff to allow a CO to move an adult to a specified place to interview him and/or to have him medically examined in private. The council can then decide whether the person is an "adult at risk" and, if so, whether it needs to do anything to protect that person from harm.

The evidence required for this order is that there is a lack of privacy to conduct an interview or a medical examination in the adult's place. The order is valid for 7 days, beginning the day after the order is granted. Technically, therefore, it could be used for 8 days. The assessment itself must be carried out in the shortest time feasible, taking into account the principle of least restrictive action. It would be good practice to detail in the application how long the assessment is expected to take (s 13; s 11(3)).

Attorney

A legal term stemming from the Adults with Incapacity (Scotland) Act 2000 but referred to in s 53 of this Act. The person granting the power(s) of attorney has full capacity and is termed the "granter". The person who is granted the power(s) is called the "attorney" or "proxy". He can have a combination of three powers – welfare, property and finance. There are two kinds of attorneys: (i) continuing attorney for property and finance powers; or (ii) welfare attorney, beginning only when the granter loses capacity (s 53; and AWI Act, ss 15–24, now amended by this Act, Pt 2, s 57). See also "Welfare attorney" below.

Availability and suitability

This is one criterion for granting an assessment order and a removal order. The council should obtain a written agreement from the owner of a specified place if this were, say, a private home, to confirm the owner's willingness to receive the adult for up to 7 days. The council is legally obliged to provide information only on the place where both orders will be carried out. It may, however, be prudent to comment on the suitability of the person who owns the place. Police checks should not be ruled out, using the co-operation duty in s 5 (s 12(c): criteria for granting an assessment order; s 15(1)(b): criteria for granting removal order).

Banning order

A protection order granted by a sheriff to ban a named person called "the subject" from being in a specified place where an adult is for the time being. The banning order can last for up to 6 months (s 91(1)).

Six additional measures can be attached to a banning order. They are: (1) banning the subject from being in a specified area; (2) authorising the ejection of the subject from the place/area; (3) preventing the subject from moving anything from the specified place, such as furniture); (4) directing the protection of property and/or requiring or authorising any person to do, or to refrain from doing something; (5) imposing any specified conditions to protect the adult at risk from the subject; (6) an open clause for the sheriff to make other conditions as the sheriff thinks necessary.[1] These can be single or combined measures attached to the order, depending on the application (s 19(2)).

When considering an application to ban a child, this should include prior consideration of making a referral to the

---

[1] The Latin phrase for this power is *"ex proprio motu"*, meaning "of one's own accord".

Children's Reporter where it is believed that there would be an effective case to answer. If the circumstances are such that there is a need to act urgently, then a referral should be made at the same time as the application for an order. Section 30(2) relates only to where the police have already arrested a child under the power of arrest.

Breaching a banning order

A breach takes place when the subject of a banning order fails to comply with the banning order itself under s 19(1) and, where attached, any of six conditions in the order listed under s 19(2).

There are two types of breach, depending on whether a power of arrest is attached to the banning order. Where a power of arrest is attached, a constable then has discretion in deciding when an order has been breached, using s 28. If not attached, then a civil action can be raised through the court, by the applicant or the adult.

In both cases, with or without a power of arrest, if the subject entered the specified place and assaulted the adult, the related criminal charges would take precedence over the breach of the banning order. The order would continue alongside the separate charging process. The sheriff might see the breach of the order as an aggravation of the assault (s 28(1): arrest for breach of banning order).

The Act details only procedures for a breach that has an attached power of arrest. An order without an attached power of arrest takes longer to reach the court. It may therefore be prudent to give sufficient evidence to ask the sheriff to have a power of arrest attached to all banning orders (s 25; Code of Practice, Chapter 11, paras 59–63).

Care Commission

The Scottish Commission for the Regulation of Care (s 53).

Child

A person under the age of 16. Children can be the subject of a banning order or a temporary banning order. See separate guidance above under "Banning order".

Conduct

This includes neglect and other failures to act, by either omission or commission (s 53). This is linked to offences by bodies corporate (s 50).

Confidence and trust

These are referred to in the criteria to dispense with an adult's consent in implementing any three of the protection orders. The court applicant has to produce evidence that there is "undue pressure" from another person in whom the adult at risk has confidence and trust. This pressure may stem either from the person harming the adult at risk or indeed from another source, such as a relative, neighbour or friend[2] (s 35(4)).

The assumption of confidence and trust may begin with a hierarchy of bonding in human relationships, starting with parent–child, siblings, partnerships and finally friendships. The assessment of this bond would depend on the development of the relationship and how the present harmful circumstances have changed this into undue pressure for the affected adult to refuse consent to a protection order (s 35(4)(a): consent of adult at risk). For further discussion, see "Undue pressure" below.

Constable

This is the police officer who will implement a warrant to enter. Warrants are attached to a s 7 visit and also protection orders. More than one police officer may be involved in using a warrant. This will depend on the risk to either the adult or others at the scene of the warrant (s 37(1): warrant for entry).

A constable can use a power of arrest when a banning order is breached (ss 28 and 29).

Continuing attorney

This means an attorney that endures that after the person who granted the power of attorney loses capacity. For further details, see "Attorney" above.

Council

A council is constituted under the Local Government (Scotland) Act 1994. References to a "council" in relation to any person known or believed to be an adult at risk mean the council for the area where the person is currently located (s 53).

Council nominee

A person who accompanies a CO when carrying out a statutory duty in the Act, ie a visit, an assessment or a removal order.

---

[2] Code of Practice, Chapter 9, paras 23 and 24, for assessment orders. The same guidance is applied for removal and banning orders, ie in Chapter 10, paras 26 and 27; Chapter 11, para 44.

The term "nominee" is specifically used in the assessment/ removal order section but they can be the same person used for interviews and medical examinations under ss 8 and 9. The term used then is "any person accompanying the officer".

Ideally, this nominee should be a professional the adult knows, for example community care/day care/care home staff or a community nurse. They do not need to have the same prerequisite qualifications as a CO. See separate terms for discussion (s 11(1)(a): assessment order; s 14(1)(a): removal order).

Council officer

An individual appointed by a council under s 64 of the Local Government (Scotland) Act 1973. The term must, where relevant, also be interpreted in accordance with any order made under s 52(1) (s 53).

There are two types of CO, depending on the duties performed in the Act, ie (1) social services worker – manager of day care services; (2) social worker, occupational therapist, nurse. Both types have to be formally registered with their professional bodies and need to have at least 12 months' post-qualifying experience of identifying, assessing and managing adults at risk (SSI 2008/306).

Court day

A weekday (Monday to Friday) unless it has been designated a "court holiday". Each court can have different court holidays. These days also do not necessarily coincide with local authority public holidays (s 53(1): Interpretation of "court day").

The Act refers to court days in calculating the number of days for which a subject who has breached a banning order can be detained (s 34(1)).

Doctor

A person fully registered within the meaning of the Medical Act 1983 (s 53).

Expiry period of 7 days or less

This relates to the period of days for which an adult can be removed from his place, using a removal order. A removal order can last for up to 7 days. The first day begins the day **after** the sheriff grants the removal order. A "day" in the order is defined as 24 hours. The adult can therefore be moved on same day the order is granted but this does not count as a period in the order itself. The same reasoning applies to the 7-day assessment order period (s 14(2): removal orders; s 11(3): assessment orders).

Fiscal

The procurator fiscal (s 53).

Functions under this Part or otherwise

The context of this phrase is after a s 7 visit investigating whether or not to implement this or any other legislation, to protect an adult at risk from harm. Parallel legislation could be, for example, incapacity/mental health/social work/housing/ police law (s 7(1)).

Harm

This includes all harmful conduct, for example physical; psychological; unlawful conduct that adversely affects the victim's finances or material possessions; or conduct that causes self-harm. See Chapter 1 for discussion (s 53).

Health professional

The designation of doctor, nurse, midwife or other person prescribed by the Scottish Ministers. These professionals are tasked with carrying out a medical examination of an adult at risk and summarising health records for a council officer (s 9(1)(b); s 10).

Local authority

The council (s 53 under definition of "council").

Moveable property

This refers to property owned by the subject of a banning order or temporary banning order. This could mean the subject's furniture, personal effects or even animals (s 19(2)(d): banning orders).

Moved person

This is the same as the specified person now being protected by a removal order: in other words, the adult being harmed (s 14(1)(a) and (b): removal orders).

Nurse

An individual registered by virtue of qualifications in nursing (s 53).

Officer in charge

This is the officer in charge of a police station to which any subject is taken after breaching a banning order (s 29(1) and s 53). See also "Breaching a banning order" above.

Parental responsibilities and rights

This refers to the situation where a child has breached a banning order and is subject to a power of arrest. The child's parents or guardians have a right to be informed of this arrest immediately (s 30(2)).

The terms "responsibilities" and "rights" are defined in the Children (Scotland) Act 1995, ss 1 and 2, as follows:

"Responsibilities": to safeguard and promote the child's health, development and welfare; to provide direction and guidance to the child; if the child is not living with the parent, to maintain personal relations and direct contact with the child on a regular basis, and to act as the child's legal representative.

"Rights": to have the child living with him or otherwise to regulate the child's residence; to control, direct or guide the child; if the child is not living with him, to maintain personal relations and direct contact with the child on a regular basis, and to act as the child's legal representative.

Person

The term "person" is used in the visits, assessment and removal protection orders, meaning anyone aged over 16 years. The term is then linked with the legal definition of "adult at risk". The purpose of the visits and the assessment orders is to establish whether a person is an adult at risk. The removal order, on the other hand, already establishes this definition (s 7(1) linked to s 4: visits; s 11(1): assessment orders; s 14(1): removal orders).

The term "person" is also used as the focus for a medical examination. This is in contrast to the term "adult" in s 8 interviews, which refer to anyone found in a place being visited under s 7 (s 9(1): medical examinations; s 8(1): interviews).

Person to safeguard ("safeguarder")

This is an option available to a sheriff before considering granting any protection order or variations of a protection order. The sheriff can specify any terms for this role, for example to focus on the application of the principles in an order or issues about consent.

The safeguarder is usually a solicitor or a social worker and appointed to act independently on behalf of the court. He has access to any agency involved with the adult and is mandated to safeguard the adult's interests (s 41(6) and (7): Applications: procedures).

Place

This term includes either the place where a person is being visited or one to which he is taken for an assessment order or a removal order. The Act interprets it as meaning "the area which the person is for the time being in". These interpretations are discussed separately below.

(i) *Visit*: A CO undertaking a s 7 visit can enter any place at the investigation stage. This could be the person's habitual residence, ie their own home or a care home. Alternatively, the person could be in any public, private or commercial premises; using social work resources such as a day centre; or be having a temporary stay in a hospital. The interpretation of "place" should therefore be broad based. See Code of Practice, Chapter 5, paras 9 and 10 for examples of places.

(ii) *Assessment orders*: The place in this context is specified in the order. The purpose is to conduct an interview or a medical examination. The Act does not specify the nature of the place except that it has to be "available and suitable". This will vary for each application but could be a local authority or a health resource. This does not prevent more informal places from being used, such as a family home. The adult's wishes, least restrictive and benefit issues stated in the Act's principles should be taken into account before deciding on a place.

The place may differ during the assessment period, depending on the purpose: for example, going to a hospital for a more complex examination. The Code of Practice, however, suggests that once the person is taken from a threatening environment, they may relax and agree to an interview (s 7(1); Code of Practice, Chapter 9, para 19).

(iii) *Removal orders*. The word "place" in a removal order is qualified by the term "specified". The purpose of a specified place in a removal order is to protect the adult from further harm.

In contrast to visits and assessment orders, the single word "place" is not used in the removal order section of the Act. The implication is that the council in its court application could use the definition "the area for which the person is for the time being", referred to above. It may be, for example, that the adult will be moved about by a suspected harmer before they can be located, hence the need for an open-ended application (s 14(1)(a): removal orders).

Power of arrest

A court document attached to a banning order or a temporary banning order on application to the sheriff at any time or, preferably, at the time when the order is granted. It allows a constable to arrest the subject of the banning order if he has breached the order or any of the six measures included in the order.

The granting and the use of the power of arrest are discretionary. The power authorises any constable to remove the subject with force if necessary, usually to a police station (s 25: powers of arrest; s 28: arrest for breach of banning order; Code of Practice, Chapter 11; paras 33–35). See also "Breaching" above.

Primary carer

The individual who provides all or most of the care and support for the person concerned. This could be a relative or friend and therefore does not include a paid carer from, say, a local authority (s 53, which cross-refers to s 329 of the 2003 Act).

Property

This could mean, for example, the adult's place, any house contents, personal effects, vehicles and animals (s 3(1)(a): adult's property).

Protection order

These are three types of order in the Act, granted by a sheriff in Scotland. They are an assessment order; a removal order; and a banning order or a temporary banning order (s 11; s 14; s 19; s 21).

Public body

These are listed in s 5(2), as follows:

(a) the Mental Welfare Commission for Scotland;
(b) the Care Commission;

(c) the Public Guardian;
(d) all councils;
(e) chief constables of police forces;
(f) the relevant Health Board; and
(g) any other public body or office-holder as the Scottish Ministers may by Orders specify.

Reasonable force

This term links to any warrant attached to a s 7 visit, an assessment order or a removal order. It allows a constable to open lockfast premises or to assist a CO to in carrying out any of these three powers, such as restraining any person (s 37(1)(a): warrants for entry).

Reasonably suspects

The evidence that any constable needs in order to be able to use a power of arrest attached to a banning order. This could be from the adult, a social worker or anyone who has witnessed the subject of the banning order arrive at at the adult's address or breach any of the six measures included in the banning order (s 28(1)(a)).

Even one eyewitness and an admission from the subject would be sufficient evidence to permit use of the power of arrest. The subject may no longer be at the adult at risk's house but have gone elsewhere. There must also be sufficient credible evidence that the order has been breached. Any evidence must be corroborated, ie more than one source of evidence (s 28(1)(a): arrest for breach of banning order).

Relevant Health Board

This is in relation to any council and means any Health Board or Special Health Board that exercises functions in relation to the council's area (s 53).

Removal order

This is a protection order granted by a sheriff, authorising a CO, or any council nominee, to move a named person to a specified place within 72 hours of the order being made; and the CO to take reasonable steps to protect the moved person from harm. The order can be for any specified period for up to 7 days after it is granted. The assumption is that a "day" means 24 hours (s 14(2)).

Representations

These are made where a person acts on behalf of another in court. This person is usually a solicitor for parties such as the council, the adult, or the subject of a banning order. In the case of a banning order, any person entitled to occupy the place concerned also has a right to representation. It would be for the sheriff to decide whether the representation was relevant to the application. The representative has to present evidence to challenge or support the application (s 41(4): legal rights before protection orders are granted).

Serious harm

This means a type or degree of harm that, in the sheriff's opinion, merits a course of action that is reserved for instances of greater danger to the adult. These include the three protection orders. The seriousness of the harm will therefore relate to how it affects the adult at risk. Evidence would be specific to the type of harm, for example physical and mental harm – medical; psychological – eyewitnesses, recording what the harmed adult says; property, rights or interests – evidence from banks, credit card companies etc.[3]

Specified

This term is used in various places in the Act in relation to any order or warrant. It qualifies a noun and so should be interpreted in it proper legal context within the Act. The following are examples where this term is used in sequence within the Act.

(i) **Specified person**: Any person living in Scotland who is aged over 16 years and who fulfils the triple criteria for an adult at risk under s 3 of this Act. The term is referred to in assessment orders and in removal orders (s 11(1): assessment order; s 14(1)(a): removal order).

(ii) **Specified place**: This is where an adult is taken to in terms of a removal order (s 15: removal order).

(iii) **Specified time**: This is part of the conditions that may be built into a removal order where contact is allowed between the adult at risk and a specified person,

---

[3] The use of the term "serious" is one for legal judgment. It is therefore for the court to arbitrate on this, particularly where a protection order is challenged by, say, the subject in a banning order.

presumably for social or rehabilitation purposes. The period could be hours and then qualified to be a lengthened or shortened, depending on the purpose of the contact (s 15(2)(a): removal orders).

(iv) **Specified conditions**: As discussed immediately above, this is a description of the arrangements to bring an adult and any specified person together during the period of a removal order. The principles of benefit, participation and the adult's wishes should help in planning any contact arrangements. This prevents the adult from feeling isolated. A social care plan may be a useful tool to guide the sheriff through the issue of specified conditions (s 15(2)(b): removal orders).

(v) **Specified place**: This applies to a warrant for entry and refers to premises occupied by an adult at risk. The place may have to be forcibly opened by a constable if access is refused. The place will also be named in Form 35 of the warrant (s 37(1) – warrants for entry; SI 1999/929).

(vi) **Specified place**: This refers to the location in a banning order where the person being banned (the "subject") is not allowed to visit. The specified place means where the adult at risk lives, possibly on a permanent basis. Alternatively, it could be where the adult at risk spends part of the day, for example in a day centre or at a relative's home (s 19(1): banning orders).

(vii) **Specified area**: This could mean the surrounding district in close proximity to the place where the adult at risk lives. The term "vicinity" qualifies this term (s 19(2)(a): banning orders).

(viii) **Specified person**: This refers to the person responsible for carrying out a task, called a "specified measure" in the banning order. This could be a CO or a council nominee (s 19(2)(d): banning orders).

(ix) **Specified measures**: This refers to a measure in the banning order to look after a subject's property while being banned. These measures are sanctioned by the sheriff, for example storing the subject's valuables or, where necessary, animals (s 19(2)(d): banning orders).

(x) **Specified conditions**: These are supervised arrangements set out in a banning order, to promote between an adult at risk and the subject of the order, so as to resolve the reason for the harm. This is further explained in s 19(3) (s 19(2)(e): banning orders).

Subject

A person of any age who is allegedly harming an adult. Section 30(2) includes children, presumably over the age of 8 years when they can be referred to the Reporter to the Children's Panel system (s 19(1): banning orders; s 30(2): if a child breaches a banning order).

Subject of the application

This is a generic term in the context of court procedures where the application is for any of the protection orders. The subject will therefore vary (s 41(3): Applications: procedure).

Summary ejection

One of the banning order powers is that the subject of such an order can be forcibly removed at the start of the order if he refuses to leave the adult's place. The police are involved in implementing this measure (s 19(2)(b): banning orders).

Temporary banning order

This is an order granted by a sheriff pending determination of an application for a banning order. It may contain the same provisions as a banning order and expires when recalled **or** when the sheriff determines the banning order application **or** is legally required to determine on it (under s 19(3)) **or** any specified expiry date – whichever of those is the earliest (s 21(4)).

Undue pressure

This is any negative influence from a suspected harmer, or any other significant person, towards an adult at risk, with the aim of having the adult refuse to consent to a protection order. The term used to define this relationship is the "confidence and trust" the adult has in this person. The legal judgment made is whether this confidence and trust relationship inhibits the adult's ability to consent. If the court decides that this is the case then the adult's consent can be ignored and the protection order granted. The assumption would be that the adult is freer to consent when he is separated from the subject by using a protection order (s 35(3): consent of adult at risk).

In contrast, undue pressure could be from a person whom the adult does not trust and who is harming the adult, for example by using threats. The third source of undue pressure could be a person not suspected of harming the adult, for example someone placing undue pressure on the adult not to

consent, or even perhaps trying to cover up for someone else
(s 35(5); Code of Practice, Chapter 9, paras 22–24).

Vicinity

In a banning order, this could mean the district in a town or
city where the adult lives, instead of banning the subject from
the entire town or city itself. The wording of this measure in
the banning orderwould depend on local geography and on
the sheriff's ruling (s 19(2)(a): banning orders).

Visit

A visit by a CO exercising a right of entry under s 7 (also
termed a "visit"); s 16 (moving an adult using a removal order);
or s 18(2) (entering a moved person's place to remove property
for safekeeping). The term "visit" also applies to using warrants
for entry (s 53(2)).

Warrant for entry

A court document that authorises a CO to visit any specified
place in terms of a s 7 visit. A warrant can also be used along
with an assessment or a removal order. A constable would
then accompany the council officer. The warrant authorises the
constable to do anything, using force where necessary, that he
considers reasonable towards fulfilling the object of the visit
(s 37).

Welfare attorney

A legal function resulting from an agreement between an adult
and someone he trusts, to decide on welfare issues should
the adult lose their mental capacity. The agreement between
the adult ("granter") and the person ("attorney") is called
a "power of attorney".

Before signing the document recording the agreement, the
adult has to confirm that he has considered the circumstances
required to trigger the power of attorney. The most likely one
would be medical confirmation of incapacity. However, the
adult need not stipulate any medical examination in the power
of attorney document. There may be an informal agreement
between the adult and the trusted person (s 53; Adults with
Incapacity (Scotland) Act 2000, ss 16–24).

Well-being

This is part of the criteria to decide whether an adult is an
"adult at risk" using s 3. This would be decided on an individual

basis and should be interpreted broadly. The general and guiding principles in the Act should help to establish what well-being means to a particular adult (s 3(1)(a)).

Appendix 2
LETTERS AND INFORMATION SHEET ON THE ACT

The following is a list of suggestions for standard information letters. They follow the sequence employed in the Act. There is also a template information sheet on Pt 1 of the Act for those adults who are subject to its provisions.

LETTERS IN THE ACT

(1) **Section 7 (visits)**: advance notice of a visit, summarising the four provisions listed in s 36 which allow a CO to make such a statutory visit. They are: (1) visit at reasonable times only; (2) state the object of the visit and produce authorisation to visit the place; (3) examine the place and take into the place any other person, any equipment or perform any other legal action to achieve the object of the visit; (4) make it clear that any person can refuse entry for a visit but that a warrant could be used if this were necessary.[1]

(2) **Section 8 (interviews)**: the purpose of an interview could be included in general terms in the s 7 visit letter, ie that the person being interviewed has a right not to answer any or all of the questions. If a formal interview is then required during the course of the s 7 visit, the person could be asked to sign a letter to this effect. It may be prudent too to state that the person can have access to independent advocacy services[2] or be accompanied by a familiar person such as a carer or relative while being interviewed. The logistics of this interview would then change.[3]

---

[1] On s 36(5) the Explanatory Notes state: "Council officers are not authorised to use force during their visit but it does not prevent a constable with a suitable warrant for entry (see section 37) from using force. However, subsection (5) makes it clear that a person who refuses entry to a council officer, or any person accompanying a council officer, for a visit without a warrant, does not commit an offence under section 49(1)."

[2] Section 6 (Duty to consider importance of providing advocacy and other services).

[3] This approach would comply with the guiding principles of the adult's wishes, views of significant people in the adult's life and participation, as listed in s 2 of the Act.

(3) **Section 9 (medical examinations)**: similar approach to s 8.

(4) **Section 10 (examination of records)**: standard letter to any agency, requesting a record.[4] A mandate signed by adult/proxy, where possible.[5]

(5) **Section 12(c) ("availability and suitability" criteria for an assessment order)**: standard confirmation letter from the manager/person who runs or owns a place where the adult at risk is being interviewed or medically examined.

(6) **Section 15(1)(b) ("availability and suitability" criteria for a removal order)**: standard confirmation letter from the manager/person who runs or owns the specified place where the adult at risk is moved.

(7) **Section 18(4) (inventory of the adult's moveable property in a removal order)**: standard letter and/or form addressed to subject, itemising the property.

(8) **Section 19(2)(d) (inventory of the subject of the banning order's moveable property)**: standard letter and/or form addressed to subject, itemising the property and safekeeping, with subject's co-signature.

(9) **Section 19(2)(a) and (b)**: a statutory duty under a banning order to identify a plan which clearly identifies the area specified in the application.[6]

(10) **Section 26 (notifications to adult and other parties after a banning or a temporary banning order has been granted)**: any applicant listed under s 22(1) – the adult, any other person who is entitled to occupy the place cited in the banning order and also the council – has to send a copy of the order to the adult/any other person as described. They must also send a copy of the power of arrest when attached.

(11) If a **power of arrest** is attached to the order, or one is later, on application, attached to the order, the applicant must

---

[4] Code of Practice, Chapter 8, para 21 suggests: "Good practice would be for each council to nominate persons of suitable seniority to have authority to make decisions regarding accessing records on behalf of the council. This decision should be made with relevant bodies responsible for keeping records such as general practitioners."

[5] Code of Practice, Chapter 8, para 14 suggests: "Wherever possible, and insofar as practicable the adult's consent should be obtained." See also paras 15–17 for further guidance.

[6] SSI 2008/335, para 2, amending SI 1999/929, r 3.35.3(1).

also send copies of the power of arrest and the order to the chief constable in the area where the subject is being banned.[7]

(12) Any applicant has to prove that they have sent the documents listed above to the court, by completing a "**certificate of delivery**". This is a statutory form called Form 34 and is in Sch 1 to SSI 1999/929 (inserted by SSI 2008/375, amended from SSI 2008/335).

(13) If the banning order or temporary banning order is varied or recalled using s 24, the sheriff clerk will notify the other parties, including the chief constable if a power of arrest is attached. This independent notification has been added to safeguard the adult at risk, as the subject of the original banning order is now entitled to apply to vary or recall the order.[8,9]

(14) **Section 41(2) (letter to the sheriff requesting dis-application of the notifications to parties, including the adult at risk, of a protection order application)**: this exemption applies to court procedures in a range of applications including specified conditions of a removal order in s 15(3) and banning orders in s 19(4). The letter could therefore be attached to the application summarising the evidence or placed in the body of the application.

(15) Section 41(3) requires an applicant (council) to **notify** the subject of the application and the adult at risk about applications for protection orders. This includes applications to vary or recall removal orders and banning orders or temporary banning orders.[10]

---

[7] SSI 2008/335, para 2(2), which amends r 3.35.4 in SI 1999/929, to include the chief constable but only when a power of arrest under s 25 is attached to the banning order or temporary banning order.

[8] SSI 2008/375, para 2(3), which amends r 3.35.5 in SI 1999/929, ie substitutes the sheriff clerk for other legal professionals for s 26(1)(b) orders only. The applicant still has to notify the parties where an order is granted (s 26(1)(a)).

[9] The list of eligible applicants to apply to vary or recall a banning order or temporary banning order is extended in s 24(3)(d) to "any other person who has an interest in the adult at risk's well-being or property". The sheriff clerk would only notify that person if they were applying to vary or recall the order. The other parties are already aware of the original order.

[10] Note: the council only needs to notify these parties about the application. The sheriff, on the other hand, has to invite the parties to court and state their right to be legally represented under s 41(4) and/or be accompanied by a friend, relative or any other person chosen by the adult in s 41(5).

INFORMATION SHEET ON THE ACT: SAMPLE TEMPLATE

This is a summary information sheet on separate aspects of the Act: visits, interviews/medical examinations, examination of records and the three protection orders. This template is comprehensive to allow for editing, and delivery is in the first person in order to give it a more personal flavour.

There has been published a simple guide with illustrations, "An Easy Guide to Part 1 of the Act", written by the Scottish Consortium for Learning Disability on behalf of the Scottish Government (2008): http://www.scotland.gov.uk/Resource/Doc/1095/0059478. pdf.

(1) **Purpose**. The Act was passed by the Scottish Parliament in 2007 and came into force in October 2008. It allows any local authority council to offer support and protection to people in Scotland who may be harmed by other people known to the adult.

(2) To do this work, the Act includes working principles for councils and other professionals such as the health and police authorities to follow. They are: to consider your wishes; to listen to the views of other people linked to your life; to help you participate in options available in the Act by giving you information about the Act; not to use the powers in the Act in a way which would discriminate you against others in the Scottish population.

(3) The Scottish Government only allows the council to use support and protection measures in the Act if you can be defined as an "adult at risk". This term has three legal tests, all of which must apply. They are listed in s 3 of the Act, as follows:

  (i) The adult is unable to look after their own well-being, property or other interests.
  (ii) The adult is at risk of harm (see separate definition below).
  (iiii) The adult's medical condition makes them more vulnerable to harm. The medical categories are disability, mental disorder, illness or physical or mental infirmity.

(4) The Act defines "harm" as conduct by a person, of any age, including children, which causes:
  (a) physical harm;
  (b) psychological harm such as fear, alarm or distress;
  (c) unlawful conduct linked to the adult's property, rights or interests such as theft, fraud, embezzlement or extortion;

(d) conduct by another person that causes the adult to self-harm, for example an adult with dementia unwittingly putting himself in danger because of an inadequate care package in his home; or self-harming as a consequence of the other forms of harm listed above.

These categories of adult at risk and harm are deliberately broad so that the powers in the Act can support and protect a wider range of people in Scotland.

(5) If a council hears about an incident of harm, it has distinct duties and powers to act on this information. First, it can make **inquiries** if it receives information from any source which suggests that an adult in Scotland is being harmed, no matter where they live.

The next duty is to investigate whether or not this information is accurate. To do this, a council appoints a council officer with legal powers to **visit** any place where an adult is living or happens to be, for example their home, in lodgings or even in public institutions such as a care home or a hospital. In other words, there is no limit on where a council can instruct its council officers to visit.

The Act lays down four provisions the council officer has to follow while doing a visit, ie (1) visit at reasonable times; (2) state what the object of the visit is and show identification; (3) examine the place for evidence of harm and take any other person with him and, where necessary, suitable equipment to that place to establish whether any harm has been done to an adult; (4) a CO cannot use force to enter any place. In other words, the adult can refuse entry. If the CO thinks the adult may still need some form of support and protection, however, he can ask a police constable to assist him. It may be that the adult is being prevented from seeing the CO.

Alongside this council power to visit are two other powers that follow on from the visit. They are first to **interview** an adult and any person in the same place as the adult, whether or not they are suspected of harming the adult. Second, the council can bring a health professional such as a doctor or a nurse to **medically examine** the adult in private. The purpose of both powers is to establish whether the adult is an adult at risk and whether they are being harmed.

Finally, the council can approach any agency which holds health, financial, or other records relating to an adult it suspects of being an adult at risk and being harmed. This is to assist it in its investigations. The Code of Practice for the Act, however, makes it clear that, wherever possible, the council has to seek permission from the adult to use these powers. They would also be used only with the permission of a senior officer within the council.

(6) An important right for an adult at risk is their consent to the use of the powers described above. The adult can choose not to answer any or all of the questions a council officer may ask in an interview and also refuse to be medically examined. In other words, the council cannot force any power in an adult's life without his consent. The important issue is the adult's need for support and protection.

(7) If, after making inquiries through a visit and then an interview or a medical examination, the council thinks the adult requires protection that is more formal, then it can apply to the local sheriff court for any of the three protection orders available in the Act. Each has a different purpose but with the overall intention of preventing further harm to an adult.

The three protection orders are:

   (i) **assessment order**: to take the adult from where they are living to another more private place, to be interviewed or medically examined. This is to assess the adult to see whether they are an "adult at risk" and, if so, whether they are also being harmed. This order can last for up to 7 days, depending on the adult's circumstances, for example living at a remote location in Scotland;

   (ii) **removal order:** to move an adult at risk from a serious source of harm. This can also last for up to 7 days but a shorter period where appropriate;

   (iii) **banning order**: this effectively bans a person of any age, including children, from doing further harm to an adult at risk. This order can last for up to 6 months. The police can step in, using a power of arrest, if the banned person tries to go near the adult at risk.

Other facts about the above three protection orders:

(1) Both the removal and banning orders can have conditions attached to allow the adult supervised contact with the person harming them. This could be where there is an attempt to resolve problems that led to the harm in the first place.

(2) As stated above, the adult has to consent to the council applying to the court for these orders. If the council,

on the other hand, believes that the adult is being pressured by a person in whom he has confidence and trust not to agree to the court application then the sheriff has the discretion to ignore the adult's consent on the basis that he would have consented had he not been pressured in the first place.

(3) In relation to the banning order, only an adult himself or anyone entitled to live with the adult can apply independently to the court to have banned someone the adult knows and who is harming him. The council would probably support that adult to make the application.

(4) The adult is entitled to be legally represented in court and also to be accompanied by anyone they choose to offer support.

Appendix 3

VULNERABLE WITNESSES (SCOTLAND) ACT 2004 – APPLICATION IN PROTECTION ORDERS

The court procedures for the three protection orders require the applicant, including the council if it has a default position under s 22(2), formally to notify the adult of the application (s 41(3)). This notification in turn triggers a letter from the sheriff clerk inviting the adult to be heard by, or represented before, the sheriff (s 41(4)).

Given the nature of the application, the adult may fulfil the criteria for being a "vulnerable witness" under the Vulnerable Witnesses (Scotland) Act 2004 ("VW Act"). This means that the court can offer measures to assist the vulnerable witness to improve the quality of his evidence. "Quality" is defined as "completeness, coherence and accuracy".[1]

The following is a summary of key information for this application, using the headings:

- Vulnerable Witnesses (Scotland) Act 2004 – summary
- Definition of "vulnerable" in Pt 1, s 1
- How to apply for special measures
- Further information on this Act.

VULNERABLE WITNESSES (SCOTLAND) ACT 2004 – SUMMARY

- This legislation is now fully implemented, with effect from April 2008. In both civil and criminal cases, it applies to any person who is defined in the VW Act as being a "vulnerable witness". The purpose of the VW Act is to enable the witness to give better evidence by reducing the anxiety and pressure he may feel while giving evidence in court.
- To this end, the vulnerable witness may be afforded any combination of the following "special measures" to use as a means of giving evidence:
  - a live television link from another part of the court building or other place outwith that building, using CCTV;

---

[1] Vulnerable Witnesses (Scotland) Act 2004, s 11(4).

- a screen whereby the accused is concealed from the witness;
- a supporter, who is a relative, lay person or professional acting in a neutrally passive role in court while evidence is being given;
- prior statements accepted as evidence-in-chief (criminal cases only);
- taking evidence on commission – by a judge or sheriff in criminal proceedings or by a person appointed by the court in civil proceedings, including fatal accident inquiries;

Note: These measures are listed in a different order in the Act, under Pt 1, s 1 for criminal proceedings[2] and Pt 2, s 18 for civil proceedings including fatal accident inquiries.

- A child under 16 is automatically entitled to "standard special measures" in criminal cases and to the equivalent special measures for civil proceedings. These are the first three measures listed above.
- The court decides all other measures for both children and adults.
- Special measures can be granted singly or in combination.
- The witness's views on special measures must be taken in account in deciding what, if any, such measures are appropriate.

DEFINITION OF "VULNERABLE" IN PT 1, s 1

The VW Act applies to children and any adult over 16 years. Section 1 defines "vulnerable witness" as follows:

"where ... there is a significant risk that the quality of the evidence to be given by the person will be diminished by reason of—

(i) mental disorder (within the meaning of section 328 of the Mental Health (Care and Treatment) (Scotland) Act 2003 (asp 13)) [mental illness, personality disorder or learning disability] or

(ii) fear or distress in connection with giving evidence at the trial."

---

[2] Part 1 of the Vulnerable Witnesses (Scotland) Act 2004 consists of eight sections that specifically refer to new insertions in the Criminal Procedure (Scotland) Act 1995. For example, in s 1 they are written as "271, 271A to 271M". The special measures are therefore in s 1(1) of the VW Act and s 271H of the 1995 Act.

Additional points:

- The reference to the quality of evidence is in terms of its "completeness, coherence and accuracy" (VW Act, s 11(4)).
- The point about the use of the word "significant" in the VW Act is that an adult may be considered as a vulnerable witness only if there is an important or material risk that the completeness, coherence and accuracy of his evidence will be reduced as a result of mental disorder or fear or distress.

HOW TO APPLY FOR SPECIAL MEASURES

- The court application can be made by any party citing a witness in both criminal and civil cases. Special measures are therefore available to defence witnesses and accused persons in criminal cases; and to all parties and witnesses cited by any party in civil cases.
- At present, special measures are not available in justice of the peace courts.
- Any party citing a witness can apply to the court for a review of the method by which evidence is being given at any time during the proceedings. The court can also decide on a review in its own discretion.
- It is solely for the court then to decide whether the witness is vulnerable and what special measures, if any, are appropriate.
- For both child and vulnerable witnesses, there are statutory application forms that can be supported by the relevant evidence.
- The court will take into account the following factors which are set out in the legislation (Pt 1, s 1(2) – criminal cases; Pt 2, s 11(2) – civil cases):
    - the nature and circumstances of the alleged offence or matter to which the proceedings relate;
    - the nature of the evidence the witness is likely to give;
    - the relationship between the witness and the accused or other party;
    - the witness's age and maturity;
    - any behaviour towards the witness on the part of the accused or any party to proceedings; members of the family or associates of the accused or such a party; or from any other person who is likely to be an accused or party to the proceedings or a witness in the proceedings;

- the social and cultural background and ethnic origin of the witness;
- the witness's sexual orientation;
- the domestic and employment circumstances of the witness;
- any religious beliefs or political opinions of the witness;
- any physical disability or impairment of the witness; and
- any other matter as appears to the court to be relevant.

- The test is the effect of the witness's circumstances on the quality of his evidence, not the set of circumstances *per se*.
- One practical way to answer these questions is to arrange a court familiarisation visit well before the first court diet.
- A suggested four-question test to prompt such an application could be:
  1. Is the witness potentially vulnerable?
  2. Is there significant risk that the vulnerability will affect the quality of the witness's evidence?
  3. What support and assistance might benefit the witness?
  4. What special measures might benefit the witness and help improve the quality of his evidence?

FURTHER INFORMATION ON THIS ACT

- The 2005 guidance pack on the special measures for child and adult witnesses is particularly helpful: Scottish Executive website: http://www.scotland.gov.uk/Resource/Doc/1099/0060018.pdf.
- L Sharp and M Ross, *The Vulnerable Witnesses (Scotland) Act 2004: Text and Commentary* (Dundee University Press, 2008).

INDEX